FOLIAGE IN YOUR GARDEN

FOLIAGE IN YOUR GARDEN

JOHN KELLY

WINDWARD · FRANCES LINCOLN

A Frances Lincoln Book

Foliage in Your Garden

Foliage in Your Garden was conceived, edited and designed by
Frances Lincoln Limited, Apollo Works, 5 Charlton Kings Road, London NW5 2SB

WINDWARD
an imprint owned by W.H. Smith and Son Limited
Registered No. 237811, England
Trading as WHS Distributors
St John's House, East Street, Leicester LE1 6NE

1 3 5 7 9 8 6 4 2

ISBN 0-7112-0506-X

Printed and bound in Italy by Lito Terrazzi

Contents

Foreword

It is my belief that we were designed to be surrounded by green, which is physiologically the most restful of colours. I am sure that this is one of the reasons for the almost universal love of gardening. It also suggests why a garden too laden with flowers is unsettling. I do not agree with those for whom foliage is everything, and who decry flowers as distractions. But a peaceful garden is basically a green garden, where foliage is allowed to work its therapeutic charm while acting as a foil and background for the stimulus that well-ordered flower colour can provide.

I love foliage. I am fascinated by the almost infinite combinations and permutations of leaf colours, shapes, sizes and characters. And I enjoy the richness of atmosphere and nuance, the never-ending changes of mood, and the biting nostalgia that foliage can evoke. The world that I should like to live in is one of blue above and *mostly* green below, which is why I am a gardener, although a modern one who likes to drive into town now and then.

I garden in a closely defined area in the southwest of England, and have just a little experience and understanding of conditions in places as different as Scotland and Florida. I can only usefully discuss plants I have known, but I would be distressed to find that in thus limiting myself I had created a restrictive impression of what is possible. My hope is that I have made certain principles clear enough for gardeners in disparate places to be able to adapt my ideas to their own environments.

I have devised a system of classification of leaves that owes a great deal to that of F.K. Makins (*The Identification of Trees and Shrubs,* Dent, 1936), but which I have modified and adapted to make acceptable to those for whom minor botanical details are, understandably, of no great interest.

Frances Lincoln is remarkable for keeping faith with a maverick author whose proclivity for sailing the more uncharted waters of horticulture must be a little unnerving. Her staff, notably Erica Hunningher, with Jo Christian, Susanne Haines and Barbara Vesey, made sure that proper courses were maintained. I would like to thank them and the genial Bob Gordon, designer of the book, for all their help.

Nicola Kelly is, I am delighted to say, my wife, and it is to her that *Foliage in Your Garden* is dedicated, with love.

John K. Kelly

Abbotsbury, Dorset, 1988

Introduction

If you were to conduct a poll among gardeners that consisted of just one question, 'What does foliage mean to you?', you would find that people fall into sharply defined categories. There would of course be those who would define foliage as 'leaves' and be quite right. On the other hand, those who understood that they were being asked to say what part foliage plays in their gardens would give a variety of replies.

At one extreme are those who would maintain that foliage is of little or no importance. These are the gardeners for whom flowers are everything. They think of themselves as growers of flowers, rather than lovers of plants, and their gardens are riots of colour throughout the spring and summer. To them the French marigold and the dahlia are the pinnacles of garden excellence and leaves are to be hidden rather than displayed.

At the other extreme is the foliage-only school. These are usually people who fancy that they are experienced and sophisticated gardeners. They tend to disparage flowers for being here today and gone tomorrow, unlike foliage which is with us all the time. Their gardens are full of so-called 'foliage plants' and there is much evidence of variegated and coloured leaves. They love catalogue entries that state that 'the flowers are of no significance and may be removed if desired'. Indeed, some of them demonstrate an obsession with green flowers.

A world of foliage, protecting, shading and encouraging the flowers. In addition to the peace it creates, foliage provides architecture, atmosphere, mood and a rich variety of shapes and accents.

No gardener is to be denigrated – people can grow precisely what they like on their own land. If a person gains all his aesthetic delight from flowers alone and another eschews flowers as unwelcome intruders, that is his business and why should anyone try to spoil his pleasure?

From the gardeners who belong neither to the anti-flowers school nor to the group involved in pure flower-gardening, our poll would reveal a tendency to think of flowers and foliage separately. Individual plants chosen for their flowers and foliage are rarely considered for their effect on the garden as a whole and in particular on adjacent plants. While some degree of balance between flowers and foliage may have been struck, it is likely that one or the other has become dominant. Most gardens fall into one of two groups, the 'leafy' or the 'flowery'. The well-integrated garden is neither: it just looks like a beautiful place, in which both flowers and foliage play their roles in the drama that is the unfolding year.

The Three Layers

Any garden, unless it is truly and deliberately two-dimensional, is in three layers or levels. The topmost one consists of trees, in scale with the size of the garden as a whole, or of a mixture of tall shrubs and trees. This is what constitutes the main structural statement and determines whether the garden is to be one of wide open spaces, deep woodsiness or one where vistas and grassy glades occur among stands of high greenery. It might, in a small, walled city garden, be made of leafy climbers trained on the walls, with just one or two small trees.

The middle level will, for the most part, consist of shrubs and, in larger gardens, of small trees. Lines of demarcation do not occur, however, and other elements will be involved. For example, upper-layer trees will contribute their lower foliage to the middle level. There will be a similar merging between the middle and lower layers, although here there will be a more discernible change. While the small shrubs and other plants of the lower level will to a certain extent be contiguous with the middle layer, there will be breaks in the continuity. Straight lines will occur where walls and hedges are, and the boundaries of lawns will intrude as well.

Only in the wild does one find that the three levels truly merge. The essentially artificial nature of a garden, with its buildings, boundaries, paths and general neatness, makes this not only impossible but also undesirable. What should be aimed for is a compromise in which the links between the foliage of the lowest level and that above are made sufficiently often and strongly enough to give an overall impression of a continuum running from the grass of the lawn right up to the tops of the tallest trees. At the edge of the lawn, prostrate junipers, whose horizontal branches rise 60cm/24 in or so from the turf, and the lowest of which sweep over the grass, would pick up the green and lift it away from the flatness. Behind them, forms of *Chamaecyparis lawsoniana* – upright, but rather open in texture – would continue the upward thrust of foliage into the middle layer, where they would find themselves in company with large deciduous shrubs and other, complementary, evergreens.

At another point, a mixed border of herbaceous plants and shrubs could be planted so that elements of it came very close to the lawn. *Alchemilla mollis, Genista pilosa*, alpine phloxes, and the blue grass, *Festuca glauca*, with other, similarly lowly plants, would encourage the sweep of the eye from the lawn, through the gradually increasing heights of the lower level, to the background of shrubs with their attendant climbers, and then swiftly up to the treetops. It would be a mistake to visualise this gradation of foliage too much in terms of the vertical. Some gardens, especially very small ones, may need to have their foliage layers disposed one directly above another, so that curtains of foliage are created. In anything larger than a minute city garden, in which great artfulness is needed in order to create the illusion of space, the rising components of the levels may in fact lie at considerable distances from one another in the horizontal plane.

You may want your garden to be viewed primarily from the house and from the patio or terrace in front of it. Your golden-leaved *Robinia pseudoacacia* 'Frisia' (and you have only one; its presence is too strong to allow for more), standing as a lawn specimen not far away, is a middle-layer plant by reason of its size, but here, because of its closeness to the observation point, it becomes in effect a member of the upper layer as well, and will relate to much taller trees that are at a greater distance, provided that they can be seen from the same point. If you wish to create such a relationship, say with a specimen of × *Cupressocyparis leylandii* 'Castlewellan Gold', you will have to design your garden so that the eye can take in both trees at the same time. What this means is that the cypress must be at the end point of a long, unobscured vista. Similarly, *Picea pungens* 'Koster', a small, intensely blue form of the blue spruce, planted close to the terrace, is a component of the upper and middle levels as you view it. Another, sited at the end of the garden, is in the lowest as well as the middle level.

Returning to the example in which junipers lay along the lawn's edge, with *Chamaecyparis lawsoniana* forms above them, it can be appreciated that there could be a considerable horizontal distance between the two. That distance will, of course, be occupied by other plants, many of which will appear above the line of the junipers. What seemed to be a simple and rather stark, if still effective, arrangement can now be seen to be one of infinite possibilities, where all kinds of foliage and flowers can form part of the picture. They will not necessarily detract from what you have tried to achieve; indeed they will only do so if you have not taken them into account. They should make the whole planting an integrated and interesting one. Gardening with foliage demands of the designer that the garden shall be planned as a whole. It is as pointless to think only in terms of the vertical as it is to visualise the garden as being completely flat. Once you start to take foliage into account, the effects of distance, of little interest to the flower gardener, become of the utmost importance.

The three levels of foliage are a most useful concept in designing, but like any other formula they must be used in conjunction with other factors. Most of all we must remember that plants are living things. They will grow and they will change, and they will be subject to the seasons.

The Two Foliage Seasons

Winter is a short season in the well-organised garden, unless the climate is a very cold one or one in which winters are prolonged beyond the usual length for temperate areas. There is a lot that happens in what we normally think of as winter that really belongs to the horticultural spring, and a good garden will often be seen as one in which the seasons merge. The period during which deciduous trees are bare of leaves is not only considerably longer than the meteorological winter; it is a great deal longer than the gardening winter. It is, then, rather difficult to talk about the bare-branched time of, say, *Sorbus aucuparia*, without having to refer to 'late autumn, winter and early spring', and still less easy with a horse chestnut, or buckeye, whose leaves fall earlier than those of most other trees.

Similarly, leafing-up starts in what we call spring, but what is, in fact, quite late spring as far as plants are concerned. Many woodland plants will have made leaf growth, flowered, and even set seed before the leaves come out on deciduous trees. Snowdrops, aconites, *Cyclamen orbiculatum* and several primulas will, for instance, be well over by the time this happens. Leaf-fall, too, is not a thing that happens simply in the 'autumn'. The term 'fall' is much more useful, but it has come to mean the same as autumn and no longer relates just to the period of colouring and falling of the leaves of trees and shrubs.

To try to describe the seasons in terms of foliage, or foliage in terms of the accepted seasons, makes for circumlocution and inaccuracy. What is needed is something that applies just to foliage that will allow us to avoid the false impression that is given by saying 'winter' when we mean half of autumn, the winter, and half of the spring. The answer lies in the distinction between the gradual and the sudden changes in the annual story of deciduous foliage. The two sudden changes – leaf fall and bud-break – neatly split the year into two foliage seasons: one during which deciduous shrubs and trees do have their leaves, and the other during which they do not. In parts of Australia, the year is split by sudden changes when the weather turns from dry to wet and back again. The rainy season is there called the 'Wet'. It seems appropriate to follow that example and to call the two foliage seasons the 'Warm' and the 'Cold'.

The sudden change between the Warm and the Cold is but a moment in the year's parade of colours, but it is the brightest and one to be treasured. The garden should not be built around seasonal colour, but autumn may be enjoyed and celebrated for the brief glories that it brings.

DESIGNING WITH FOLIAGE

Every garden is different, not only because of its climate and soil, but also because of the personality of its creator or of its present owner. If it is a good garden – a place of harmony, beauty, balance and year-round interest – it will have been designed according to sound principles, but it will be governed by personal preferences as well as practical possibilities.

A great many of us find ourselves with new gardens consisting of more or less rectangular areas of mud left by the builders. Some people acquire houses surrounded by neglected, overgrown gardens in which there may be one or two good plants and a few desirable ones. Others take over an existing mature garden, in which all kinds of habitats for plants have already been made. Whatever the state of the garden, we are unlikely to find a design that suits its unique circumstances, and the trouble with treatises on garden design is that they tend to present a static picture. Everything is seen on a sunny spring or summer day when no winds blow, and no dark clouds threaten the idyllic scene.

In these theoretical gardens, no slimes grow on the neat paving; the drips from overhanging leaves do not create muddy patches on the pristine lawns. But some days are sure to be dull and depressing and we should take account of that. When the wind lashes the flowers into submission and the rain makes them hang their heads, will our garden be something to turn away from? Or shall we be able to look out of the window and admire the silver flash of a poplar, the shiny solidity of a holly, or the slow wave of the flag irises beside the pool? And when the sun comes out, will it illuminate the startling whiteness of *Cornus controversa* 'Variegata' set before a backcloth of deep green, or have we put it on the wrong side of the green, so that such an unforgettable scene is never to be ours?

Many people allow the plants to set the atmosphere because it is for their associations with one another that they have planted them. Others will deliberately set out to create a definite mood. High, evergreen trees, deep greens and a predominance of large leaves with brakes of bamboo set at the turns of narrow paths, walled-in by lushness, appeal to those who like mystery and an ambience that verges on the subtropical. More open spaces and airy foliage convey a lighter spirit. With a splash of gold here, a shine of silver there, a cloud of diaphanous smoke over a cotinus and the dancing leaves of an aspen, the garden will seem almost to float on air.

Whatever the daemon of your particular garden, it is the successful use of foliage that can banish it. The flowers may well fit into the genius of the place, but it is the foliage that sets the scene. Climate, soil and the available plants allow us to make an almost infinite number of choices so that we create gardens that are highly personal but which nevertheless obey certain principles of design.

In this peaceful corner there are shrubs, climbers and herbaceous plants, variegated and plain leaves, spiky and rounded shapes. Every kind of foliage is represented, from the misty puffs of asparagus to the tropical-looking leaves of the loquat, Eriobotrya japonica, *by the pillar.*

There are principles that can be applied to all sizes of garden and to all but the most desperate situations. Gardening with foliage requires that all normal factors of cultivation, as well as seasonal changes, are considered, but with a much deeper understanding of the plants themselves and in particular of the leaves that constitute foliage.

The Interplay of Foliage

The first respondents to our poll told us that foliage meant 'leaves'. It does, of course, but it means more than that. Foliage is a collective noun for leaves; it refers to a population of them on a plant or on a collection of plants which, while in place, constitute foliage but which, once they have fallen, become merely leaves. The effect of foliage is determined either by the shape, size and colour of the individual leaves or by the inter-relation of leaves *en masse*. This may seem to be a distinction without a difference, but an example or two should show that it is not.

The Chusan palm, *Trachycarpus fortunei*, has fan-shaped leaves that can be as much as 90cm or 1.2m/36in or 4ft across, each one a dramatic scene-setter, evoking subtropical climes, even though it is as hardy as old boots. Planted next to *Podocarpus salignus* (a conifer that looks nothing like one's idea of a conifer, but which is clothed to the ground with dense, billowing masses of tightly packed, dark green, narrow leaves) the subtropical aura is enhanced, even though this combination is possible where temperatures fall as low as -12 °C/10°F

The few leaves – perhaps thirty or so – carried by a twenty-year-old Chusan palm make a superb contrast against the foliage of the podocarp, which may consist of many thousands of leaves. Each leaf among the thousands is of little account compared to the mass, but each frond of the palm stands on its own in the composition of the picture.

This distinction becomes particularly important when it comes to placing plants whose effect depends on the size or density of their leaves. In the above example, the size and shape of the palm leaves should never be obscured, even in part. If the palm were to be planted behind the podocarp, only a hint of its majesty would peep through the swatches of the conifer's foliage. On the other hand the conifer loses nothing by having part of its amorphousness hidden by the palm. Neither its overall shape nor the nature of its foliage is lost.

It is, then, a general principle of designing with foliage that large, bold leaves should be in front of small, massed ones. The sharp observer will, at this juncture, point out that such an arrangement will contradict itself when viewed from the other side. So it will, but surely the matter is solved when another palm is planted so as to be at the front when viewed from this new position. Far better, though, to use something else like a catalpa or *Fatsia japonica* and to walk right round the conifer, enjoying the variety.

The effectiveness of large, bold leaves against small, massed ones is evidenced by this planting.

Large and bold leaves

Large leaves are not necessarily bold, nor bold ones large. Another dubious distinction? Hardly. Take the case of *Fatsia japonica* and its hybrid versus the common ivy × *Fatshedera lizei*. *Fatsia* leaves are usually about 40cm/16in across and can be more, while the hybrid's are seldom greater in width than 10 or 12cm/4 or 5in. Both have strong shapes and are glossy and grown for their foliage effect. In the open garden (× *Fatshedera* grows larger in its parts as a house plant) they are both bold-leaved plants but, in comparison with so many other things, the ivy-hybrid does not have large leaves, while *Fatsia* certainly does.

Fatsia japonica is, like the Chusan palm, grown largely for the subtropical aura suggested by its large leaves. That both are bone hardy has nothing to do with it; it is leaf size that counts. Nothing in gardening affects the ambience like large leaves do, whether by accidental placing or by intentional design, so they should be used with great care. This is not an injunction as to their use, but a plea that their due respect should be given to them.

The dramatic effect on the mood of a garden afforded by large-leaved plants cannot be exaggerated. Just a few hardy subjects could make a garden in which one might imagine oneself deep in some exotic jungle. The 2m/7ft canopies of *Gunnera manicata* on their stems of that height, lurking magnificently by a small pond and accompanied by the similarly-shaped but barely 60cm/24in leaves of *Peltiphyllum peltatum*, packed

In this planting the large, bold leaves of Petasites japonicus *and* Hosta sieboldiana *are used to dramatic effect.*

together like an army of shields, would set the scene. Nearby, the massed umbrellas of *Magnolia tripetala* would rise some 6m/20ft, allowing some sunlight to filter down to the massive, dark green canoe-paddles of *Rhododendron sinogrande*. A carpet of *Petasites*, the winter heliotrope, with leaves like so many discuses hiding the soil, would run up to the bases of the Chusan palms; the trunks of the palms, clothed in ready-woven, fibrous sheets, would be decorated with the variegated form of Canary ivy.

Such a garden is possible in all but the coldest parts of the cool temperate zones and where strong winds would not penetrate. It is an extreme example, but it illustrates the strong influence of the largest-leaved plants. With variations, it exists in many places where shelter alleviates the worst bite of the occasional severe winter.

Bold foliage, on the other hand, need not have the same sort of influence. The oriental plane most certainly has leaves that are bold, but they are saved from sheer largeness by their deeply five-lobed shape. Drama there is, especially with a large specimen, but the effect on atmosphere is not so great. The mahonias, whose stiff habit lends architectural quality to their long, pinnate leaves, are *par excellence* bold-leaved plants, but somehow one does not think of such leaves as large, neither do they conjure up the same feeling of steamy closeness.

The marbled, pointed, and seemingly endlessly varied leaves of *Cyclamen hederifolium* are not large; each is not much bigger than that of the hornbeam that may grow above it. They are, though, most definitely bold in character and serve to make the point that, along with such plants as the petasites, largeness and boldness have their place and their usefulness at all levels of the garden, from the highest trees to within a few centimetres of the ground.

ABOVE LEFT Gunnera manicata, *not yet at its full summer height, suggests an aura of mystery, its lush leaves calling to mind far-off, exotic lands despite the traces of frost that linger on it leaves, as yet untouched by the early-morning sun.*

ABOVE RIGHT *The broad, three-lobed leaves of* Arisaema candidissima *appear in early summer after the flowers have made their entrance.*

Leaf density

The density or sparseness of what we have referred to as leaf population will greatly affect the appearance of particular plants. Similarly sized and shaped leaves will constitute very different kinds of foliage according to the densities in which they occur.

Looking again at *Podocarpus salignus*, it will be seen that its foliage is, above all, dense. A well-furnished tree will not show its branch structure because of its solid masses of leaves. As a foliage tree it is useful, but only as a background. On its own it is a splodge, and a very dark green one at that. Apart from the darkness of its colour, however, if you were to take an average podocarpus leaf and compare it with one from the dragon's claw willow, *Salix matsudana* 'Tortuosa', you would find that the two are quite similar in length and width. Nothing could be less similar than the two trees.

The willow has foliage that is quite sparse and whose comparatively scattered nature means that the tree's structure is highly visible, even when it is in leaf. This is important, because it is the curious, twisted nature of the branches that makes us want to include it in our gardens. Imagine now that the salix is planted behind a similarly-sized podocarpus. It disappears from view, obscured by the dense foliage in front of it. Have them change places and the willow's strange structure can be seen and, what is more, the sparseness of its foliage does not prevent you from seeing the podocarpus.

It is, therefore, another principle of designing with foliage that plants with more dense foliage are placed behind those with less. This may seem elementary, but time after time the classic mistake is made: camellias in front of Japanese maples. This is because a young planting looks well enough arranged thus when the gardener can look down on the grouping; it is when the plants grow above eye level that the maples are obscured. Placed in front of the camellias, the maples are seen to their best advantage while not hiding their companions at all.

Yet one more principle of designing with foliage now becomes apparent: young plants must be visualised as mature ones.

Density of foliage plays a part in the effectiveness of shapes. A strong vertical accent or a rounded shape is important to composition and should be carried out with a plant whose foliage is dense. The effect is weakened if something is used that is less than solid in outline. Obviously, an evergreen, densely-foliaged conifer or a clipped holly will do the job best, but if the choice is between two deciduous shrubs or trees, then the denser one should be chosen. *Carpinus betulus* 'Fastigiata' is, for instance, of much the same size and shape as *Quercus robur* 'Fastigiata' but it is a lot denser.

A variety of dense foliage in a secluded corner of this garden. The sparser leaves against the dense, dark ones of the hydrangea enhance the feelings of repose and privacy.

Static and Moving Foliage

Many plants have leaves that hardly move at all in the wind. They are mainly, but not all, evergreen and they are usually dense. Many other evergreens are, by contrast, highly mobile, like bamboos and evergreen oaks, but in general mobility is a property of deciduous plants, while evergreens tend towards rigidity.

Apart from the purely decorative impact of movement and the momentary changes that it brings, the mobility or otherwise of leaves has a psychological effect. The heat of a summer's day may seem to be alleviated when foliage rustles and waves in a light breeze, while the same movements in winter can suggest a chilliness that may have little to do with the real temperature. Our bamboo, then, would be better sited where it can be seen from the poolside or from the lawn, rather than from the windows of the house. It can perform its cooling function while we bask outside in the summer and it can wave its chilling message unseen from within the warm house on a blustery winter's day.

A good balance of evergreen and deciduous plants will always create a degree of movement among the foliage of the garden that is neither excessive nor tending towards torpor. The result will be a combination of a feeling of stability and restfulness with a lightness and airiness that gives a garden spirit and life.

BELOW LEFT Foliage features that remain unmoving are reassuring in their solidity. They also provide shelter from strong winds, and contrast well with more mobile plants.

BELOW RIGHT Grasses react to every passing breeze – their leaves shimmering, their airy flower-heads dancing. They should be placed near more static plants.

Accent Foliage

In a well-planned garden, foliage will fall into two categories – accent and background. Even though each member of the background may be highly distinctive, it will still blend in with its neighbours to help to create a restful whole.

Against this background, accents of various strengths will occur. While it may be only a matter of one still tree among many that sway and flutter in the wind, it is more likely that accents will be created by using shape or colour. Thus, a plant with very large foliage is a major accent when seen against a background of massed, smaller leaves. A shrub with light-coloured variegation stands out more strongly with dark greens behind it, and a purple or gold-leaved plant comes in to its own when accented by neighbours in shades of green.

There are many such ways of using accents and they are what distinguish a good garden from a bad one. Without them, there is a tendency towards dullness and uniformity; too many of them and the result is an unharmonious mess. The 'foliage only' school falls into this latter trap. Their over-emphasis on what they call 'foliage plants' leads them to fill their gardens with accents. It is rather like a précis of Beethoven in which all the big, climactic chords are played one after the other with all the quieter bits left out. The result is a strident jumble in which no plant is seen at its best and where there is no rest or harmony.

Acer japonicum *'Aureum' likes enough sun to keep its colour and enough shade to prevent its scorching. In an ideal position it will stand out from its surroundings as a strong golden accent.*

The distinction that we should make is between 'foliage plants' and plants that have beautiful foliage.

Variegated plants can make superb accents, often with a hint of surprise, especially when the variegated form is found among its plain-leaved fellows. A carpet of *Vinca major* lit up with just one patch of *V.m.* 'Variegata' is a fine sight and an excellent use of foliage as ground cover. *Weigela florida* 'Variegata', whose light, grey-green leaves are margined with creamy-white, is exquisite among other weigelas or with shrubs of similar habit. Overdo the variegated plants, though, and each one loses its individuality and its capacity for creating an accent.

Among the most telling of accent plants are those that have sharply ascending foliage. Fastigiate, conical and cylindrical shapes are to be found among evergreen and deciduous trees and shrubs alike. The foliage scene in general is one of indeterminate, billowing shapes, and such definite structures lend order and punctuation to the picture. The same effect is achieved at lower levels by plants whose leaves are sword-shaped, or whose leaf stems arise from the ground vertically. By the waterside, *Iris pallida* 'Variegata' strikes a strong note among the pleated leaves of hostas and *Veratrum nigrum*. Its handsome leaves, like bundles of sabres, stand sharply erect. And yet, with nothing like the uncompromising pointedness of the iris, the arum lily, *Zantedeschia aethiopica* 'Crowborough', rises strongly upwards as well. Its light green leaves do not have the spikiness of the iris; they open out at the top into flattened canopies and are so different that the two can be planted together without overstatement. To place the irises next to other spiky things like phormiums would be overdoing things, but its juxtaposition to the arum lily is an example of contrast within a contrast, a device which reinforces an accent planting without being too obvious.

Aromatic foliage

There is a certain time of the year – not quite summer, but almost after spring – when you suddenly sense that the air is filled, not with scents, but with aromas. You realise all at once that the atmosphere has been flat for months. What has happened is that the warmth of the sun has reached the stage when it becomes capable of causing the leaves of plants – not just a few, but a great many – to release substances that affect us in a way that makes us recognise them as aromas. Unfortunately our sense of smell is such that it soon becomes overloaded by persistent odours and the effect is lost until a day comes when the sun is so hot and the air so still that the concentration of evaporating oils and esters becomes strong enough for us to be aware of them again, wafting gently all around us on the still air.

Of course, by this time it is likely that we shall be assailed by the perfumes from the flowers, and these will come and go against the aromatic background in just the same way as the blooms that give rise to them pass their fugacious lives against the constancy of foliage. Although this general background is made up of a myriad of elements, including the weak but pervasive aroma of growing grass – quite different from that of grass when it has been cut – and the indefinable but definite scent of rain at a distance, there are plants that have very strongly scented leaves. Some of them produce aromas that are very pleasant, while others, mercifully few, are attractive enough

RIGHT *The ashy-grey leaves of the lavender find their echo in the foliage of* Cedrus atlantica *var.* glauca, *the stately blue Atlas cedar. The lavender's aroma heightens the more usual visual and tactile joys afforded by a garden.*

BELOW *Aromatic herbs – represented here by a pleasing combination of purple sage and* Origanum vulgare *'Aureum' – make a valuable contribution to the scented air of the garden.*

in flower and leaf appearance to be garden-worthy but are positively revolting in the olfactory sense. Their placement is vital if we are to enjoy the former for their aromas and the latter for their visual characteristics alone. While it is, perhaps, of the first priority that plants should find their best roles and positions as elements in the foliage picture as a whole (taking into account, of course, their flowers) it is a strong secondary consideration that we make the most of the scents of their leaves, and that we should be able readily to reach those plants whose leaves we want to use in the kitchen.

Any foliage in the upper layer that is aromatic must be left to get on with assisting in the general sweetening of the air. We are only going to be interested in plants that are growing where we can reach them, which is to say in the middle and lower layers. Since reaching them is desirable, aromatic plants are best grown near paths. This is not merely so in the case of herbs and *Laurus nobilis*, the culinary bay, but also with such things as *Eucalyptus* species, leaves of which might be plucked idly in passing to be carried about during the rest of one's walk round the garden and dropped only when one had tired of its powerful but refreshing aroma.

The volatile oils and other substances in plant leaves have been made use of for centuries in cooking and in freshening homes. This is a practice that will never die and such things as sage, rosemary and fennel will always be grown for the pot and will always be a pleasure to have growing near the house, where they may readily be picked, no matter what the weather. Lavender, too, whether the traditional 'old-fashioned' lavender or *Lavandula stoechas*, the French lavender (a plant too tender for gardens with severe frost) will never lose its popularity as one of the least cloying of all scents. On the other hand, nobody who has grown

Foliage and flowers in balance. Delphiniums contribute their own distinctive foliage as well as their noble purplish-blue flower stems while Alchemilla mollis *makes a frothy show at their feet.* Sambucus racemosa *'Plumosa Aurea' echoes the yellow of the alchemillas and makes a superb backdrop for the colours of the delphiniums.*

Clerodendron bungei will ever forget the skunk-like reek of its handsome leaves when they are only mildly disturbed. However, it can be grown to great advantage under rhododendrons and other shrubs whose flowers have finished by autumn, as it will grow up through them and lend them its viburnum-like heads of rose pink flowers whose scent, paradoxically, is magnificent. *C. trichotomum* var. *fargesii*, a more shrubby, tall plant, has delightful white flowers and turquoise fruits, but a place where it may be discreetly viewed and not smelled is advisable, as it is for the tender *Cestrum* species, beautiful in flower, but rabidly foul in foliage.

The Role of Flowers

While it is true that good gardeners choose individual plants for their flowers and their foliage, they usually forget to consider the mutual effects of adjacent plants. For example, the green of a large rhododendron can be fairly dull. Set in front of a copper beech or other purple-leaved shrub or tree, such as *Prunus cerasifera* 'Pissardii', it becomes part of a pleasant contrast. If, however, the rhododendron is 'Moser's Maroon', the grouping will be strikingly and unusually effective while the rhododendron is displaying either its coppery young growths or its deep maroon flowers. Try it with 'Peter Koster', the trusses of which are a brassy magenta, and the whole thing becomes an excruciating mess.

Concentrating too hard upon foliage effects and on plantings that use delightful combinations of foliage without taking into account the effects that the flowers will have upon one another is to miss the boat completely. To illustrate this, I will cite a ghastly mistake of my own. It occurred to me that the grey, rather woolly leaves of the herbaceous perennial *Lychnis coronaria* would benefit by contrast with the sword-like, sharply ascending, light green leaves of *Crocosmia* 'Lucifer'. That this was an error engendered by being half frozen while planting would be a charitable way of looking at this dreadful blunder, because the horrendous clash between the red-purple of the lychnis and the shrill scarlet of the crocosmia was truly heroic. Had I, chilled to the marrow though I was, remembered the true colours of the flowers, I would have shuddered inwardly and planted something entirely different.

Shapes of flowers should be taken into account. A formal, highly developed sort of bloom is unlikely to harmonise well with a simple, single flower that is unchanged from the wild. A white-flowered camellia, clothed to within 30cm/12in or so of the ground with shiny, broad foliage, might look very well with *Kerria japonica* planted just in front of it and pruned every year after flowering to keep it short. The matt, small, light green leaves would be an interesting foil for the glossy dark green of the camellia. If the flowers of the camellia were single and natural-looking, the match would be felicitous, as the yellow flowers of the kerria, appearing at the same time, are similarly simple. Formal double camellia blooms, with many petals packed into symmetrical rows, would make the combination look out of place, but with the double flowers of *Kerria japonica* 'Pleniflora' the balance would be restored.

Viburnum plicatum *'Mariesii' is noted for the 'wedding cake' tiering of its branches. This is never more emphatic than when each branch is picked out in flowers, just as though the cake has been iced. The soft pink spikes and lettucey leaves in the foreground show that the dock family also has much to offer. Other plants nearby gain from their proximity to these lovely flowering plants.*

The foliage-only movement can be seen for the truly negative force that it is when we consider plants that have beautiful flowers as well as lovely foliage. One such is *Cytisus battandieri*, the pineapple broom from Morocco. In any garden it would be an asset for its leaves alone, as they are so covered with fine, silky hairs, tightly adpressed to the surfaces, that they appear to be plated in silver. It is a tall, slim shrub or a small tree and loves the warmth of a south-facing wall, even though it is hardy. Its flowers, borne in midsummer, are bright yellow and are held in tight heads that are shaped more like those of a lilac than of a broom. What is more, they carry a scent of pineapples. That anyone should consider the flowers to be of no importance is beyond belief.

On a smaller scale, the same applies to the low-growing shrub *Convolvulus cneorum*. This, again, is silver-plated, and its white, trumpet-shaped flowers are likely to be seen on the plant for most of the year unless a very cold winter intervenes. It is just not possible to grow this for its foliage alone; its flowers are so distinct, distinctive and persistently borne that it must be placed with neighbours that will benefit from association with both its foliage and flowers.

Foliage can be so arranged as to be a celebration of a flower. One of the best and most unusual examples I have seen was in a corner of a large garden, but could have been transported into a small one with no loss of dramatic effect. A bush of *Cotinus* 'Notcutt's Purple', a dense mass of quite small, deeply red-purple, rounded leaves stood against a wall. In front of it was a planting of *Senecio cineraria* (syn. *Cineraria maritima*), whose almost white, flannelly leaves made a startling contrast around its feet and just to one side. To the other side and curving round behind the senecio was a small drift of the dahlia 'Bishop of Llandaff'.

This dahlia has foliage that is the same colour as that of the cotinus, so that, when it was not in flower, the arrangement was a simple one in which the white and the purple leaves made an interesting, if slightly obvious, statement. The flowers of the dahlia, though, are of the purest, most brilliant bright red. When the Bishop bloomed, the flowers seemed suspended against the background of deep, blackish red and appeared almost to float above the white leaves. The designer had combined an annual with a tender perennial and a hardy shrub, and had used the dahlia's own foliage to combine with the other two to create a frame and a canvas upon which to display one kind of flower in one colour at just one time of the year. That he understood the art of balance was obvious; what he had in addition to that understanding was the sort of flair that makes a gardener great.

The Foliage Balance

When we compared the leaves of *Fatsia japonica* and its hybrid with common ivy, × *Fatshedera lizei*, we concluded that, whereas those of *Fatsia* could certainly be termed large, those of the hybrid could not, although both are bold. This was all right as far as it went, but fell short of the truth because it took no account of scale.

In a corner of a very small garden, where a partly sunny corner is made by two stone walls, a small-leaved, variegated ivy, such as *Hedera helix* 'Gold Heart' climbs and scrambles up the walls. A dwarf willow, *Salix helvetica*, a rounded, bun-shaped mass of silvery, woolly foliage that looks as if it would make a most comfortable pillow, makes a striking but quiet contrast. Around it and covering a couple of square metres of the encroaching paving is a dense sprawl of × *Fatshedera lizei*, occasionally reaching up as if to assist the climbing efforts of the ivy. None of the three is dominant; it is a balanced, harmonious, restful, cool corner. The balance is achieved by the juxtaposition of a small-leaved plant with brightly variegated leaves, another one with small leaves, but this time covered with silky down, and one with plain green leaves which echo the shapes of the ivy foliage, but which are much larger. In this arrangement, the hybrid's leaves definitely look large, and yet we earlier took them as an example of those that are not. The apparent contradiction is explained by the phenomenon of scale.

The principles of designing with foliage apply to the smallest place in which foliage can be grown as well as the very largest. The three layers of foliage will exist and interact just as much in a courtyard garden behind a busy city street as they will in the broad acres of a country property. This comparison is, though, another over-simplification, because scale is also a factor *within* each foliage layer. The levels can be and often are represented on a smaller scale within a particular level.

LEFT *Balance achieved in the association of four distinct kinds of foliage. The large, bold, simple, glossy leaves of the* Rhododendron macabeanum *(the pure white, cottony undersides of the newly emerging leaves can just be seen) find something in common with the much smaller but glossier simple shape of the camellia. Total contrast is made with the fern,* Dryopteris borreri, *whose fronds are not too delicate for the company they are keeping. The Japanese maple is the perfect background.*

RIGHT *Balance need not mean obsessive tidiness. Here many different kinds of leaves contribute to make this an interesting and visually satisfying scene. Would the wall look as old and comfortably set if the grass at its feet were cut?*

OPPOSITE A town garden. Many motifs and styles are possible when walls enclose small areas – they are certainly not automatically limited. Lushness such as this departs from the austere angularity we associate with the city.

BELOW A typical cottage garden, in which what seems to be a jumble turns out on closer acquaintance to be the product of considerable art.

Geoff Hamilton, a friend and a well-known gardening writer and broadcaster, has a garden in which design has been developed to a fine art. The grand sweep of the garden is a mass of flower colour and interesting structures, all afloat on a sea of fascinating foliage combining beauty with practicability. There is no place within it, no matter how small or seemingly insignificant, where the design becomes weak. Although it covers 10,000 square metres, nobody could accuse Geoff of not knowing how to garden on a small scale. Adjoining his house is a delightful cottage garden, surrounded on all sides by walls the colour of bleached honey.

The cottage garden has its own upper level, composed of small trees, including the Kilmarnock willow, *Salix caprea* 'Pendula', and some medium-sized shrubs, most of which would, in a larger garden, be middle-level members. The middle level here, though, is made up of smaller plants, such as the denser, hummock-making hebes. It is, however, within and among these levels that he has created foliage arrangements in miniature, each one complete and integral in its composition. One such is so effective that I found myself unable to help coming back to it again and again. Growing to about 90cm/36in on one of the walls are the narrow bands of pure, light yellow of the ivy *Hedera helix* 'Buttercup'. They thread their way over the sunny stone like broad veins in its substance, bright, soft gold against the tawny stone. Beneath are three low-growing, grey-leaved plants – the silvery filigree of two artemisias shimmering besides the more staid business-grey of a phlomis.

These are the upper and lowest levels of this grouping, but where is the middle one? This is the touch of sheer genius. *Hedera helix* 'Buttercup' has pure yellow leaves, but only when they are young. Those that are older, and that tend to gather into a gradually proliferating mass lower down, become suffused with green as they age. The middle layer is therefore of an infinite variety of variegated leaves, including some that have turned quite green.

The lowest level of foliage, that which is far and away the most neglected in the majority of gardens, here contains within itself all the principles of designing with foliage – three levels, contrast of form and colour, and a consciousness of flowers and related plantings. In what respect are these last two principles carried out? In yet another brilliant way, in which the element of surprise, so vital a part of the best gardens, is brought into play: the flowers of the phlomis are pure, bright yellow!

Character and scale are inseparable. Most of the foliage in this cottage garden consists of small leaves, and the shrubs – evergreen *Ceanothus, Kolkwitzia amabilis*, weigelas, and so on – are entirely appropriate in a cottage setting. Large foliage is supplied by hostas, hellebores, and other species that fit into the ambience, and there is no false note that might jar the eye. It would be quite wrong to plant one of the really large-leaved rhododendrons, such as *R. macabeanum* in this garden; the heavy, jungly note would be com-

pletely out of character, as would *Fatsia japonica*. *Rodgersia* leaves, like shiny, exaggerated versions of those of the horse chestnut, look fine nestling among the shrubs, but not those of *Gunnera*.

On the other hand, a garden of identical size, bounded perhaps by higher walls, set behind a Victorian house, could become a place of mystery and exotic romanticism if it were filled with large-leaved, jungly plants – just those that would be out of place in the cottage garden. This is not to say that all the foliage should be large – the principles of design still apply – but their largeness should be emphasised by comparison with smaller ones. Weeping fuchsias, the pinnate fronds of ferns, trifoliate clematis, and heart-shaped *Lapageria* would be among the lesser foliage elements that would match the mood, and these would provide flowers that were in character, too.

In the larger garden, the necessity for planting in groups arises if scale is not to be violated. One plant of *Helleborus foetidus* may well make an extremely powerful statement about itself in a small garden, but in a large one its voice would be lost. To be heard, it may need to be present in a drift of a dozen or more. In the context of group planting, a 'larger' garden is simply one that is not the smallest. The average-sized home garden will benefit from having one or two subjects planted in drifts – a group of Japanese azaleas of compatible flower colour will become an undulating cushion of green later on, among which lilies may grow and lift their flowers above the low-growing foliage. The bigger the garden, the more it will be desirable to plant in groups. The groups, too, will themselves be larger.

The Warm and The Cold

The two foliage seasons give us two contrasting 'pictures' to look at, and provide us with a tool for planning gardens with both deciduous and evergreen elements. They make it easier for us to switch in our minds between the Warm and the Cold.

Imagine that your house has a garden that is rather large. It starts out flat and slopes upwards, providing a clear skyline (you are lucky and have no neighbours in that direction). You visualise a planting of conifers of various kinds with rhododendrons and azaleas for spring colour, but you would like a really strong group of deciduous trees to provide a touch of drama in the autumn as the leaves colour up. Your taste tells you that this would be a more pleasing prospect than if you interspersed the deciduous trees freely among the conifers and rhododendrons.

While this image is in your mind, you have been using a vision of the Warm. Now switch seasons. Suddenly there is a huge gap in your otherwise green or coloured picture. If you were planning to have the deciduous trees near the skyline, you will now see that there would be a large breach in the trees which would be filled with branches in silhouette. It would forever niggle you with its appearance; it will look as if some blight or fire had struck to spoil an otherwise rich picture. With your mental picture of the Cold, move the belt of deciduous trees downward so that they nestle among the evergreens. Switch to Warm and see how their leaf tones will create a 'different' note and how their leaves will behave differently in the wind from those of the conifers. Look again at Cold and you will be able to visualise the coral stems of maples, the blue twigs of willows and the white stems of birches all showing their true colours because they are seen now with a background of green and are not reduced to black outlines against the sky.

Balance in a garden is about many things and their interaction, but what really determines the overall character of any garden is the ratio of deciduous subjects to evergreen.

The evergreen/deciduous balance

A garden with a superabundance of evergreen conifers will have a cold feel to it; it will be redolent of montane heights or of high latitudes, while a predominantly deciduous garden will appear quite cosy until the Cold, when it will become very chilly indeed and, what is more, will lack movement.

Where there is a very high proportion of evergreens of the non-coniferous kinds – for example where an attempt has been made to create a jungly, sub-tropical atmosphere – there will be an absence of change that will lead eventually to boredom, and the opportunities for creating surprises with flowers and with scenes revealed only during the Cold will have been lost. Furthermore, although gardens in the far south of the United States or in the Caribbean get away with being preponderantly evergreen, they do so because the Cold, such as it is, is a time when the flamboyant flowers of hibiscus, bottlebrushes, and bougainvillea bloom beneath a bright blue sky. Heavy canopies of dark green merely emphasise the leaden skies of the Cold in higher latitudes; the trees and shrubs cringe in snow and frost and show their unhappiness at being thrashed about by rain-laden gales. There is none of the sheer glory of hoar-frost on deciduous branches and twigs; that magical moment when the low winter sun lights them up from behind and the expelled breath of wonder hangs mistily in the still air.

The gardener in a temperate region who uses his imagination to create a balance between evergreen and deciduous does not aim merely at compromise. He seeks to design a garden in which the one discipline complements the other. A temporarily sad group of camellias will act as a green curtain against which the bright red branches of *Acer palmatum* 'Senkaki' can be seen in all their glory. The silver frost on a crab apple's

ABOVE Evergreen and deciduous elements combine to form a beautiful summer scene. Dark olive greens and bright yellow greens cast shadows on the mown path; silvery reflections play on the water's surface.

RIGHT The same garden prepares for winter. The deciduous canopy begins to drop, allowing the winter sky to be seen above the formally arranged evergreens. The winter structure of this garden is emerging intriguingly and greatly different from the summer one although the same elements are present.

branchlets is all the better traced by being outlined against a holly, and a chilly, small garden can have its moment of fire when *Acer palmatum* 'Heptalobum Osakazuki' burns scarlet against a hedge of *Lonicera nitida*.

Every deciduous subject has to be looked at as if its foliage were suddenly gone, and the result examined critically. What is left? Is it an unacceptable gap? A shapeless tangle of unruly twigs? And what has it revealed that has been lurking behind it while it was in leaf? The mobile but small leaves of the Himalayan birch, *Betula jacquemontii*, are not out of the ordinary, but their character is such that they combine well with the stillness and much darker green of *Arbutus unedo*, the Killarney strawberry tree. During the Warm, this is a pleasing, if not spectacular combination.

Switch to the Cold. Suddenly, there is a pure white tracery of elegant branches arising from a smooth, snowy trunk, all outlined to perfection against the darkness of the evergreen. Not only that; there is a hint of mystery – of fusion – because the extremities of the birch's branches are dark brown, so that they seem to disappear within the substance of the arbutus.

It is by no means only among woody plants that the absence of foliage becomes marked during the Cold. There is not much that can be done about the traditional herbaceous border when all the plants go to sleep; a stark, rather muddy patch remains, with little tufts of attenuated sticks and lonely labels looking like a battlefield after the war has moved on. But it is much better in the case of the mixed border, where the shapes and structures of shrubs, that were obscured to a large extent by their ebullient cohorts, are revealed.

The largest herbaceous plants, gunneras and the tallest grasses, such as *Miscanthus sacchariflorus*, leave, in the badly planned garden, ugly gaps. If they are grown so that they actually hide scenes of interest, such as garden statuary, cascades, or short vistas, the Cold will be made that more refreshing by the transformation that results. Alternatively, their absence may redound to the benefit of evergreen plants, or of deciduous ones with interesting forms which might not otherwise have been seen from the particular direction from which they now become visible.

Seasonal colour

The Cold and the Warm are the seasons of major changes; along with these the minor ones have to be remembered as well. Possibly the most telling minor change is a very gradual one; the darkening of foliage colours as the Warm progresses.

Spring leaf colours are, among deciduous plants, bright and fresh, with a hint of gold in many of the greens that helps to make spring such a bright and joyous time. These greens become more similar to one another as time passes, so that the darkest of them become quite dowdy and the brightest ones, on the whole, rather more sombre. An extreme example of this is *Acer pseudoplatanus* 'Brilliantissimum', whose spring foliage is of a bright shrimp pink. Unfortunately, its broad, lobed leaves become dull green quite quickly and are soon no different from any old seedling of *Acer pseudoplatanus*, whose leaves are as dull as ditchwater. It is, nevertheless, a popular small tree, which goes to show that its moment of glory looms far too large in the minds of gardeners.

An appreciation of the effects of time on the green tones in the garden will lead us to the inescapable conclusion that we should try to plant things whose foliage will be bright green in the late summer, when uniformity has taken over. These

The snowdrops and hellebore flowers tell us that it is spring, but the crisp freshness of their leaves alone would tell us this as surely. The marbled foliage of Arum italicum *var.* pictum *sets off the more pure green of its associates.*

can be either deciduous or evergreen, but they should not be overdone. A garden in which all the trees and shrubs looked spring-fresh after mid-summer would be one in which mutton had been dressed up as lamb.

Oaks that have reached the greybeard stage, and limes, whose leaves are being sooted by the mould on the droppings of the aphids, will be cheered up by having as a neighbour the evergreen *Griselinia littoralis*, whose bright, apple-green, shiny, quite mobile leaves remain youthful throughout. The ordinary, green *Robinia pseudoacacia* has a verdant freshness about it that has been quite forgotten since the advent of its golden cousin, but it is an ideal foil for stately but serious conifers, or for dogwood trees, whose leaves not only become extremely boring in summer, but also subject to a disfiguring fungus disease.

The middle level will contain its proportion of dull greenery. Anyone wishing to grow *Philadelphus* for its beautifully scented flowers will have to admit that there is only one that has foliage of merit. This is *P. coronarius* 'Aureus', whose leaves are of a light, buttery yellow, becoming slightly green as they age. It is not really among the ranks of golden-foliaged plants by late summer, but has become foremost among those that can recall the golden-green of spring.

The wonderful reds and golds of Acer palmatum *'Heptalobum Osakazuki' form only part of this autumn scene. Its green neighbours contribute an evocative sombreness that is peaceful rather than sad.*

RIGHT When autumn colour is used with discrimination the results are truly dramatic. This Japanese maple has been placed carefully so that its beautiful ruby-tinted leaves will be shown to best effect, especially when touched by the sun.

LEFT Many plants have colourful foliage for much longer than the autumn. Cotinus coggygria *undergoes subtle changes in tone all year long, offering constant interest and variety.*

The large, lettucey, deeply-cut leaves of the tree peony, *Paeonia lutea* var. *ludlowii*, are of a green that looks bright and fresh enough to eat. Seen next to a stiff, prickly, dark green holly, these leaves are magnificent, but it is worth growing one or two more so that they can cheer up the dowdiness of *Magnolia* × *soulangeana*. A large plant of the peony will not be dwarfed by the magnolia, neither will the bright yellow, frilled flowers interfere with the purple-stained, white ones of its neighbour, as they appear when the others are over.

The short interregnum between the Warm and the Cold – the autumn – is a time when everyone sits up and takes notice of foliage. Exoduses to Vermont, or to the great arboreta of Europe, demonstrate the impact that the flaming colours of autumn have on everyone who loves a good spectacle. There is nothing wrong with this. It is, after all, an easement to the soul to feast one's eyes on beauty, and autumn colour certainly has no time in which to pall or to provide surfeit. The problem is that in the eyes of most people it has come to be the only time of the year when foliage is noticed, other than as a sort of amorphous, peaceful, green overblanket beneath which the flowers snuggle.

Too much attention to autumn colour has led to an almost complete absence of stress upon leaf colour at other times of year. Much is heard about gold, grey, purple and variegated leaves, but what garden centre emphasises spring foliage, unless it is to describe the unusual, such as *Pieris*, or the freakish, like *Acer pseudoplatanus* 'Brilliantissimum'? And it is worth a heavy wager that no sales outlet will consider it a selling point of a plant that it has leaves that are as bright a green in summer as in spring.

Indeed, so greatly is interest in foliage concentrated upon the autumn that there are now long lists of new varieties of *Pieris* in which flower colour is the great virtue, with pink blooms seeming to be *le dernier cri.* None of them has the brilliant scarlet new leaves of 'Forest Flame' or 'Wakehurst'. They all achieve merely the coppery or bronze tones that those two great varieties surpass so wonderfully. Gardeners, one is glad to say, show that they have not fully succumbed to ignoring foliage effects for spring, as they will snap up a batch of 'Forest Flame' before you have a chance to tell them that its best role in autumn is to be surrounded by blue agapanthus.

A mind trained to imagining the garden travelling through the time dimension will see autumn for what it is: a short, transitional period of ephemeral beauty. In the image of the speeded-up film of the year that results, autumn colour appears as a sudden, extremely bright, but soon extinguished flash.

It is, therefore, a fundamental mistake for the garden designer to fly straight to notions of autumn colour as soon as foliage is mentioned. It is far better to make other considerations come first and to let the autumn take care of itself. Plants such as the Japanese maples, *Malus* and *Sorbus* have a great deal to commend them besides their late leaf colour, and they should be obtained and placed for those other characteristics first. Although it is a good idea to site them so that sunlight will exaggerate and enliven their autumn tones, their places in the much longer-lasting foliage ensemble should take priority, along with the disposition of berries and flowers among the other colour elements.

Liquidambar styraciflua is a beautiful tree, with maple-like leaves and gorgeous, deep red leaves in autumn. But do you really want one in your garden? It is a large tree, it has no ornamental flowers, and it does nothing in the spring. If you have a very large garden, you might include it as a member of the upper level, but in a smaller one *Acer capillipes* would be much better. Its autumn colour is almost as good, and it has interestingly striated bark and coral young shoots – great assets in the Cold when the liquidambar looks stark.

And why grow *Parrotia persica*? Admittedly this tree, whose autumn colour comes early, would go out of cultivation if nobody were to grow it, but in many gardens it is, for most of the year, very ordinary indeed and eventually far too big. For those who have large gardens it can figure quite high on your list, but buy it for its small, hamamelis-like, bright red flowers that appear on the naked branches early in the year. The autumn colour will happen anyway, but as a bonus.

ABOVE *Awaiting the onset of autumn. The flowers linger, the trees have not yet lost their summer strength.*

RIGHT *Winter in all its stark beauty. The chilled evergreen leaves huddle beneath safely dormant branches. Are these foliage scenes any less exquisite than those of autumn?*

The gold in the leaves of this Ginkgo biloba *and the strongly emphasised structure of the new and older leaves of* Rhododendron macabeanum, *brought out by low sunlight, provide a valuable example of light and its uses. A planting, as it matures, will catch the light at varying angles, an effect the gardener can plan for once he has recognised its possibilities.*

Wind, water and light

The Warm and the Cold provide us with sharp and simple contrasts between the foliage seasons. Other kinds of changes, more ephemeral ones, complete our model and change it from a static concept to a consideration of the living garden.

Sorbus aria 'Lutescens' is one of the best of the whitebeams because its leaves are white-felted above in summer and spring. In late summer they become green on their upper surfaces but remain shining white below. Plant it in a sheltered spot and it is a very attractive tree of no great size. Put it, however, where the wind can bluster through its foliage and you will see a dazzling, constantly varying shimmer of silvery white that nobody can walk past without being compelled to stop. A strong wind turns the tree into a wave of whiteness, while a breeze flicks and teases it so that it flashes on and off like the glint of foam on the sea. Or take *Alchemilla mollis*, the lady's mantle of the border, whose rounded, greyish-green leaves are lightly hairy, but whose flowers are of no distinction. It is not a plant that provokes a strong reaction in the normal course of events but, when it has rained, it is a casket of jewels. Drops of water, held by the hairs, sparkle like fine diamonds and shiver brilliantly with every zephyr.

Camellia leaves are deliciously, richly green and glossy. They are never boring plants like laurels can be, even when their short flowering season is over. When the sun shines on them, though, their curved, shiny surfaces act like so many closely-packed small mirrors, reflecting the white sunlight in a thousand different directions, while the dark heart of the plant becomes black by contrast.

The light changes during the day and its quality acts upon the plants in subtle ways. Not all these changes can be taken into account when a garden is being designed; they mostly happen to everything all at once. A knowledge and consciousness of the effects of light, wind and water will, however, play a major part in decisions about

Alchemilla mollis *after rain, magically transformed by the droplets of water shimmering on its leaves.*

siting plants. That these factors are of far greater importance in general with foliage than with flowers is one of the reasons why the gardener who understands foliage will end up with a better garden than someone who merely places plants better to display their flowers.

Related Plantings

Ideally, every plant that you put in your garden should be in harmony with everything else. This is, in practice, an almost impossible ideal, but if it is striven for the results will approach the ideal, and nobody can do better than that. There is bound to be a bit of serendipity thrown in as well, and that is often where the magic lies. Relationships between plants will be established in the vertical plane as well as the horizontal – a copper beech in the upper level and *Cotinus* 'Velvet Cloak' on the ground is a very strong one – and they will be there whether you plan them or not. The chances are that if they are not, they will be either bad or ineffectual.

Much is heard about colour schemes or planting 'themes'. Blue gardens, silver plantings and so on are the darlings of a certain school of gardeners, many members of which are truly brilliant and accomplished horticulturists. Their ideas work very well and have been an inspiration to many who have carried out similar plans on a greater or lesser scale. When it comes to their putting their schemes down on paper, the difficulties become apparent. Conditions of climate, soil and aspect, among others, are never the same in any two gardens, so it is difficult for a scheme that works in one garden to be carried out in another. What can be done is that the general principles that underlie the scheme can, if properly understood, be applied elsewhere using different plants, or by comprehending fully the adaptability of the plants involved in the original scheme.

Planting plans are seldom understood by those who study them. For instance, there is a current fashion among those who profess to be disciples of the great Gertrude Jekyll that orange is abhorrent and pastel shades supreme. Jekyll herself used extremely strong colours, not excepting orange in its most outspoken shades, and she was not averse to employing the most vivid reds and even magenta. The whole point of Jekyll's genius with colour was that she could create, using the entire palette from the loudest to the quietest hues, an appearance of utter tranquillity. At the heart of her genius was an acute appreciation of the relationships between colours and of how plants relate to one another. If we are to learn anything of value from her it is not how slavishly to copy her plans or planting schemes, but how to understand those relationships.

It is the job of those who write on gardening, as she did so wonderfully, to assist readers in broadening their horizons so that they may plant in original and imaginative ways. It is restrictive to provide plans in the hope that they will be carried out as written or drawn. Suggestions, and not orders, are what enable gardeners to let themselves go and enjoy themselves creatively.

Every plant makes a statement about itself. That statement may be about orangeness, or roundness, or it may be a little more abstract and involve presence, elegance, or stateliness. A plant in a relationship with another will not only make a statement about its neighbour; it will say something about itself. It may emphasise the orangeness, roundness, or elegance of its neighbour by echoing these qualities or, conversely, by having completely different ones. Echoes, or statements of agreement, may be made over very short distances, or the plants involved may be far apart from one another. Generally speaking, the further they are apart, the more links or allusions need to occur between them. Take, for example, *Robinia pseudoacacia* 'Frisia'. It may be overplanted, but that is hardly its fault; it is still as good a tree for golden foliage as one could wish. Planted in front of holly, *Pittosporum*, rhododendrons (but beware flower colour!) or any dark-leaved deciduous tree, its statement of goldenness is strengthened by the dark background, especially in sun.

This statement needs no echoing close at hand, but is powerful enough to carry for quite a distance, perhaps as far as a nearby *Gleditsia triacanthos* 'Sunburst', whose foliage is of a softer gold with some green in it. The two will say things about one another's goldenness and you will find yourself noticing each a little more in terms of its true qualities. If the distance between them is too great and communication breaks down, then a shrub of *Weigela* 'Looymansii Aurea', of smaller stature than the two trees, will establish the necessary link. Because both trees are pinnate-leaved, you will have established their relationship as well. Another, nearby, with green leaves this time – it may be an ash – will pick up this part of the message and transmit it to a wisteria, whose climbing habit communicates with that of a clematis growing into the crown of soft, yellow leaves of *Sorbus aria* 'Aurea' – and so on.

A word of warning: strong statements, made with conviction, are liable to run into opposition. This was what happened when I made my ghastly error with the magenta-pink of *Lychnis coronaria* and the brilliant scarlet of *Crocosmia* 'Lucifer'. Each on its own is all right, but allow their voices to rise together and an argument ensues.

In the garden in which I am privileged to work, a catalpa has recently thrust a branch through a curtain of the densely-packed, small leaves of a large evergreen oak (*Quercus ilex*). The effect of this large cluster of big, heart-shaped leaves high up among all the little ones is strangely compelling, and I look at it far more often than at the main part of the catalpa itself on the other side of the oak. Large leaves are enhanced by massed small ones, but they can also co-operate with others. *Rhododendron calophytum* and *Gunnera manicata* can combine their boastfulness to mutual profit, but either will loom large against *Betula utilis*. A planting in which most of the leaves are small, on the other hand, needs just the odd (but very strong) mention of largeness to bring coherence and interest.

Related plantings also occur when plants are allowed to relate to things other than plants. The artefacts associated with the garden, from the house downwards, can be integrated into the garden by their relationships with the plants in it. In a warm part of the world a flat-roofed, old stone house, set upon an elevation above its garden, looked down on an old cedar tree, whose flattened top magnificently echoed the shape of the house. A series of curving steps away from one side of the pool was answered by a corresponding curve of prostrate junipers on the other, and the buttresses of the curtain wall below the house found added expression in a group of tall, straight cypresses. Throughout the garden there was not a single false note. The foliage of the plants and the structures of the home and its surrounding buildings created a scene of unforgettable peace.

The use and understanding of the principle of related plantings allow for the release of individuality in garden design. It avoids the strait-jacket of 'schemes' and it imposes a discipline on those who would fill their gardens with unrelated, clashing 'foliage plants'.

Cultivation

Gardens divide themselves into climatic types, even within the confines of the cool-temperate zone. There is the typically Cornish garden, full of rhododendrons and azaleas but nevertheless very different from one with the same plantings on the east coast of Scotland. Soil and climate will dictate differences between gardens in upper New York State and those on Long Island. The choice of plants, the poorness or richness of the soil, the strength of the local winds – all these will stamp their authority on what sort of garden you can or cannot create.

Appreciation of the requirements of plants and a deep understanding of garden design are evident in this related planting, in which blue and gold are used in interlocking relationships. Catalpa bignonioides *'Aurea' is the dominant gold note, repeated by the vertical elements and strengthened by the fuchsia.* Agapanthus *and* Artemisia *exchange blue between their flowers and foliage and echo the mixture of upright and drooping elements above them.*

LEFT Much of plantsmanship means understanding the needs of plants and putting them to grow where they will thrive. Good garden design has to do with placing plants where they will contribute most to the beauty of the garden. It is not often enough that good garden design and plantsmanship go together, but when they do the results are in a class of their own, as in this waterside planting, where water-lilies, marginals and dry plantings further from the water's edge all enjoy their sites and combine to form a beautiful and successful foliage picture.

RIGHT Sparkling health evinced by clean, fresh-looking foliage, abundant flowering and plenty of new growth is not achieved by accident. Plants have to be suited, not only to the overall climate, but also to any microclimate in which they find themselves. A sheltered, moist, humid place suits Aruncus sylvester *perfectly, so that it is encouraged to thrive and produce its white blooms enthusiastically. White-flowered, too, is* Cornus kousa *var.* chinensis, *so often made to be uncomfortable in hot sun, but relaxed and strongly-growing in partial shade.*

Climate is something with which we all have to live. It is no good recommending the feathery, grey-green foliage of the mimosa, *Acacia dealbata,* as a foil for *Paulownia tomentosa* and a companion for *Pittosporum* 'Abbotsbury Gold' unless we realise that gardeners in Newark, England, or Newark, New Jersey have grasped the idea successfully enough to try something that suits their cold winters. Similarly, one hopes that a Californian seeing *Weigela florida* 'Variegata' used as an informal hedge in England would seek the same effect using *Pittosporum tobira* 'Variegatum' which will thrive in the hot West Coast summers.

Poor soil and bad cultivation will never allow foliage to thrive, unless they are corrected. A badly-drained garden must have its drainage rectified, otherwise willows and alders will be left to fight it out with docks, nettles and the coarsest invasive grasses. Light soils must be fed with manure, compost and whatever organic material can possibly be found. Heavy soils will have to be aerated and improved, and those that are compacted or podsolised will present the inevitable physical challenge of double-digging.

It is no use trying to introduce the flaming young foliage of *Pieris* 'Forest Flame' if your land

is heavily charged with lime, nor the delicacy of Japanese maples if your soil is only a few centimetres deep and overlies oölitic limestone. The Brobdingnagian, rhubarb-like *punkah* fans of *Gunnera* cannot form part of your grand design if your garden is dry or subject to searing temperatures. No matter how clever you are at putting into practice the principles of related plantings, you will come a cropper if you pay no attention to the requirements of plants in cultivation.

Furthermore, it must never be forgotten that plants grow, and that they only grow well and carry out your design if you allow them to and give them encouragement. In gardening with foliage this is of supreme importance, for it is foliage that shows the health of a plant more than its flowers do. A plant that feels itself under threat is likely to flower very well; it is a manifestation of the imperative that drives all species to perpetuate themselves, but it will show its distress by producing fewer or smaller leaves, or both.

The failure to allow plants room to develop is one of the most common errors. It is so tempting to try to produce instant effects in a new garden that plants are often put in with little thought to the space that they will eventually occupy.

Overcrowding can, in the short run, be cured by moving plants to other sites if they are threatened by invasion by their neighbours. The time available is truly short, because trouble in the form of distortion starts soon and quickly becomes irreparable. Again, the sort of damage involved may not matter too much to the gardener who is primarily interested in flower colour. The foliage gardener, or indeed the plantsman, to whom the form of a plant is of high importance, will find the results of bad spacing to be unacceptable. Trees and shrubs that are too close together become drawn up and leggy and soon lose their lower leaves and have to have their dead lowest branches pruned off. The result is a forest of trunks and stems at just that level where there should be interesting interactions of foliage.

It is the top layer of foliage that sets up the habitats for other, more lowly plants. Trees will cast shade. They will shelter less robust subjects from the depredations of wind, extract moisture from wet soils and shade dry soils so that they do not become like deserts. Strong shrubs of the middle layer will do the same job, but their roles must be seen in the shorter term; it is the trees that determine the long-term future of the garden.

A new garden just cannot be planted up with all its inhabitants in one go. A shady bank where crowds of autumn-flowering cyclamen will one day entrance with their marbled leaves cannot appear overnight. A windless corner for the vulnerable leaves of *Acer palmatum* 'Dissectum' is not going to establish itself miraculously. Neither is it a very good idea to put *Weigela* 'Looymansii Aurea', which needs full sun to maintain its golden leaves, where a group of birches will all too soon shade it down to a half-hearted green. A sense of scale is required just as much when plants are being selected in the nursery as it is in any other aspect of garden planning. A good plant of *Sorbaria aitchisonii* may be smaller than one of *Ceanothus* × *veitchianus*, but it will very soon outstrip it and, if you have not been careful, deprive it of the sunlight it needs.

Flower gardening can be planned for the short run more easily than gardening with foliage. It is possible to achieve highly colourful gardens very quickly if hardy perennials, shrub and cluster-flowered roses and quick-growing shrubs are used. Foliage needs time to develop to a point where it becomes effective, and it needs even more time if relationships are to develop between the various elements. Your design, then, must be one in which the dimension of time is allowed to come into play. The carpet of cyclamen will have to wait – you will establish them one day – and the variegated elaeagnus whose leaves you would like to see mingle with those of a nearby silver one will have to sit by itself until it is big enough to join in.

All is not a test of patience, though. The sea of daffodils that you crave can go in now, and so can the snowdrops. Both will tolerate the sun, and they will still be there when the upper-level foliage reaches maturity. They will become denizens of the woodland, rather than jewels of the meadow. A fence may well give the shade that will later be extended by trees, and other shade-loving shrubs can be grown under the lee of a wall, a shed, or the house itself until such time as they can be moved to the places that you have planned for them.

None of this alters the fundamental necessity for thinking ahead. Garden planning that concentrates on the here-and-now and takes no account of the future is no planning at all. You don't have to leave everything until the oaks are mature, but a measure of common-sense flexibility and anticipation will go a long way.

As well as taking account of the future, we cannot afford to lose sight of the fact that we live in the garden. It is all very well establishing the most ravishing arrangements, but if they are in the way, or blot out the light from the neighbour's windows, they are doomed to a temporary existence. In the real world, convenience and use are what really determine the design of our garden. It is no good waxing lyrical about aesthetic considerations if we cannot find our way to the vegetable patch on a wet day without having luscious foliage firing icy drips down our collars – we shall soon find the axe a more desirable tool than the trowel.

Foliage that needs to be appreciated from close at hand – aromatic leaves, for example – would, one might think, be best grown near to a path. Quite so. But what one must remember, once again, is that plants grow. As the garden matures, trees and shrubs planted near to a path will begin to encroach upon it. At first you will go along and cut back the odd branch in one place and a few shoots in another. As the years go by, you will find that, in order to keep the path clear, you have to clear away great cartloads of stuff, leaving behind a neat, rather hedge-like boundary. This will not happen everywhere, nor at all points on a given path, but it will certainly happen if your garden is well-furnished with foliage. Your aromatic plant, if it is in such a position, will become unreachable because of the rigid mass of branches below it and because its lowest leaves have disappeared in the general clear-up. Where it should have been planted is where the path passes a glade, in which are perennials: geraniums, hostas, primulas and so on. There it can grow unencumbered so that its branches reach tentatively, like the questing, gentle trunks of elephants, towards just that height from which you can tweak off a leaf, crush it in your hand, and move on, taking its fragrance with you as you go.

Foliage size, shape and colour are essential factors in a pleasing design, but it is the variety of leaf density that gives a design real interest, depth and character.

LARGE TREES & TALL SHRUBS

The tallest trees are extremely important in creating the overall atmosphere of a garden or landscape. Long before you start to notice the rarities among the shrubs, the treasures that make up the colours of the borders, or the layout of the lawns and paths, you will have been affected by the impact of the trees. As you walk into a garden it is the trees that tell you whether it is a small or large one and, by their distribution, whether the atmosphere is close and jungly, open and airy, or damp and woodsy.

When looking at a large tree you are unlikely to notice its leaves, unless they are particularly large. What you observe is foliage: the mass of leaves as distinct from individual leaves. Your first impression is of shape. The massed foliage appears as an entity having a characteristic form, and this appearance of solid individuality is greater when the foliage is dense.

This is why it is so easy to recognise species of trees by their silhouettes. The Hungarian oak, *Quercus frainetto*, has a distinctively egg-shaped outline, whereas the pin oak, *Q. palustris*, is tall and slender with a high head. It is not necessary to pick leaves from them to tell which is which. Curiously enough, once you have learned what the characteristic shape of a species is, you will recognise it, if it is deciduous, even when it has lost its leaves. Just as the skeletons of an orang-outang and a man can be readily distinguished, the branch skeleton of a tree in winter is as individual as when it is covered with the flesh of foliage.

However, most of us do not know the shapes of many trees. There will be few gardeners whose knowledge would be up to telling a Bishop pine from a Monterey pine merely by their outlines. What happens when you first see a garden with large trees in it is that you register a lot of big, green shapes. It is not much more than that, especially if they really are all just green.

Suppose a large garden has a lawn surrounded by belts of tall trees, all with quite dense foliage consisting of fairly small, green leaves. What you see is rather like the surroundings of a football pitch – the shapes of the stands are obvious, but they are packed with an amorphous mass of humanity in which it is impossible to distinguish a single individual. You have an entity which is called a crowd. Sitting amid this crowd, you will find it pretty boring to spend half-time studying the crowd opposite. One sweep of the eye seems to be enough to extract all the interest that is there, but is it? If you look again you notice that there is a large block of seats occupied by supporters wearing red hats, or waving blue scarves. This is interesting, but even more so when you start to notice that there are little pockets of colour in other parts of the stand – sometimes only one or two at a time. By now you are really *looking* at the crowd opposite, and in a short space of time it has become fascinating and you may be reluctant to stop watching them and turn your attention to the return of the players for the second half.

The greatest variety of colours and shapes will be found where the upper and middle layers of foliage meet. Contrasting and complementary tree forms allow for softness and rigidity, horizontal and vertical accents, and for the association of conifers with broad-leaved trees.

RIGHT A massive lime like this so dominates even a large garden that it comprises an upper layer all by itself. Its influence on the quality of light in a garden and its overall cooling effect ensure that every other planting must be made with reference to it. A gardener who takes on a tree like this must learn to garden around it, and his first lesson will have to do with the creation of atmosphere by large trees. The seat gives the scale, and the bright flower bed beyond gives the lie to any idea that this is a sombre garden.

OPPOSITE Cornus kousa *var.* chinensis. *Although it is usually seen as a smaller specimen than this, it is an upper layer tree in small gardens, where its layered shape is a striking feature, even when not covered as if with snow by the myriad bracts of its inflorescences.*

Whether you are looking at a crowd or a belt of trees, amorphousness is boring whereas variety and action create interest. Even three similarly green trees of typical 'tree' shape will be dull to look at but each will be interesting if elements of difference and contrast are introduced. A dark green tree flanked by light green ones will stand out. Not only is its foliage of a different shade but also it has a shape that distinguishes it from the others. A purple-leaved tree introduces a new note, but it is a note sounded with true purpose if it draws attention to the much smaller purple-leaved plant lower down in the middle layer of foliage. Now your eye has started to move across the scene and you are starting to *see* the belt of trees in all its variety of shape and colour.

Just as bad as amorphousness is excessive variety. If the football stand had been filled with supporters all wearing hats of different colours and waving multicoloured scarves, there would have been nothing very interesting about the crowd. The amorphous nature of the rest of the crowd was essential to setting off the interesting elements. Similarly, the belt of trees needs its plain green areas, otherwise the whole thing will become a tiresome mess of contradicting colours, shapes, and messages. If the elements that are to create interest are made too much of, you will find that boredom has returned.

It is not just colour and shape that create interest. Even though individual leaves are not greatly important in larger trees, occasional large-leaved trees will strike a strong note and introduce a feeling of texture.

SHAPES OF TREES

The shape of a plant is usually not thought of as having anything to do with 'foliage'. This is because the difference between 'leaves' and 'foliage' is not understood, or even recognised. The shape of a plant has little to do with its leaves, each of which is an individual and is either large or small, coloured or green, and is held vertically or horizontally or somewhere between the two. It does, though, have everything to do with its foliage, the total population of leaves which may be dense or sparse, weeping or upright, rounded in billows or stiffly tabulated – or in combinations of these features.

The weeping, golden form of beech, *Fagus sylvatica* 'Aurea Pendula', does not achieve distinction because of its transitory aspiration towards goldenness – an ambition shared by many less deserving trees – but because of its outstanding shape. Its branches hang downwards almost vertically and lend it a lissomness and chic that earn it a place on the arboreal catwalk. Note that it is the branches that hang. Brewer's weeping spruce, which may be thought to owe its extraordinary form to its leaves, is in fact made so strongly lachrymose by its branchlets; thin, threadlike, woody structures against which the leaves are tightly adpressed. No leaf on this tree weeps – the foliage as a whole does. The spruce is,

The weeping beech, Fagus sylvatica *'Pendula', is a large tree of spectacular form. This specimen is only just approaching middle age. The name covers at least two separate clones, one of which has branches that are nearly vertical and the other (this one) branches that tend toward the horizontal, allowing the branchlets bearing the foliage to hang like green curtains.*

of course, an evergreen and has the same appearance and shape throughout the year. Deciduous plants, though, look very different in the Cold. Where then is the colour of their leaves? Gone, but the shapes of deciduous trees that have lost their leaves remain as the woody skeletons that support the foliage shapes in the Warm.

When choosing trees that will for many years determine the character of your garden, do not be seduced by leaf quality, but try to find out what foliage effects will be created by the trees when they grow up and evince their mature shapes. This applies as much to the smaller trees and the shrubs that will occupy the middle layer of the large garden or the upper layer of a smaller one as to the largest trees. Sometimes it is all too easy to dismiss a large tree as being of little interest, like the common hornbeam, *Carpinus betulus*, whose leaves are of no distinction and whose shape fails to lend them any. *C.b.*'Columnaris', on the other hand, is a small tree, whose shape and dense habit of growth render it a valuable addition to the foliage scene at lower levels. It is columnar while it is young and then broadens, but its leader never loses its dominance, so that it grows like a very sharply pointed egg. In the Warm, this pleasing, solid shape presents a dense mass of foliage almost like a piece of topiary. When the Cold takes over, the solidity gives way to an airy mass of short shoots which express exactly the same shape, but in a suitably wintry way.

A perfect counterpart to this is a form of the chestnut-leaved oak that has quietly insinuated itself into more and more gardens in recent years. *Quercus castaneifolia* itself is quite a large tree – it is said to grow very large, but I have serious doubts about it – whose foliage is superb. Each leaf is about 15cm/6in long and sharply and deeply toothed, and the colour is black-green. *Q.c.*'Green Spire' will be larger than the hornbeam, but it will have much the same shape – to grow the two together would provide the fascination of two trees of similar form but widely unrelated, and the great contrast between the characteristics of the similarly-shaped foliage masses. The Cold would set a difficult problem even for the most knowledgeable plantsman, however, as their differences disappear when they are leafless.

No matter the size of your garden, the largest plants in it are the ones with which the greatest care should be taken when they are being chosen. This mainly applies if you are setting up a new garden or have taken over one which is sparsely furnished, but there are occasions when some of the upper layers of plants should be removed in a garden that has been planted for a long time – here, above all, mistakes should not be made. It is a good idea to start off by visiting arboreta and gardens open to the public which are within comfortable reach of home – particularly those that you can go and see during both the Warm and the Cold.

Here you will be able to see and appreciate the shapes of the trees and have an understanding of what they will look like as they approach maturity. You will also be able to get an idea of related plantings among larger trees – how a strongly fastigiate tree planted directly in front of more billowy ones and – even better – set back into them in a bay, makes them seem further away. You may be able to work out how the designer has used false perspective to highlight some dramatic foliage effect. The brilliant red of the autumn colour of *Acer rubrum* 'October Glory' is highlighted in one garden by its being viewed down a short avenue of narrowly fastigiate trees. The distances between them lessen as the acer is approached, while the avenue simultaneously narrows. This allows the illusion of distance within a small area.

Shape is so important in large trees that it is worth taking a long time over choosing them and their sites. You can get on with other parts of your garden design while you spend if necessary a year or two becoming really familiar with the ones that are just right for you. You can also compare young specimens with mature ones – an extremely useful exercise which will, among other things, tell you that spruces and pines develop high crowns and long boles when planted in company, while cypresses, podocarps, ginkgo and yew do not, but remain well-clothed low down and can serve to unite the upper and middle layers.

In case you are taking fright at the thought of a garden in which there are such big trees, a glance at a garden in which I once lived may set your mind at rest. It was 2000sqm/half an acre in extent and contained six very tall Lombardy poplars, a huge English elm and an equally majestic Huntingdon elm, a fully mature *Zelkova carpinifolia* and a *Magnolia acuminata* of great age, an ancient oak with a tree house in it and some more elms in which there was a colony of crows. Yet the garden was by no means full of trees. Besides a good sweep of lawn there was also a tennis court.

While it is true that the average gardener, faced with planting trees in middle life, is highly unlikely to see them reach maturity, that is far from a reason to decide not to plant them. If all gardeners took the view that it was not worth growing large trees because of the length of time they take to grow to their ultimate sizes, none of us would ever see tall trees in gardens and we should all be much the poorer for it. In fact, most gardens which are large enough to contain big trees have usually had them planted at some time in the past before their present owners took them over. Owners of such gardens owe it to their predecessors as well as their successors to plant trees which will take over when the existing ones have died of old age or from the ravages of storms.

It is only a very few years before the largest trees become part of the middle layer of foliage, where they will give great pleasure as well as enhancing the leafy scene in the garden. If their planting is done with this in mind as well as their ultimate role in the upper layer, posterity will be served as well as the present generation. In a world in which the numbers of noble trees are rapidly and sadly declining, is it not the duty of all of us who can to plant the best and most beautiful of the trees that will enjoy our particular climatic and planting conditions?

Picea brewerana, *the very slow-growing Brewer's weeping spruce, is never likely to exceed 12m/40ft, but this is still tall enough for the middle layer of large gardens or the upper layer of small ones, and its great beauty demands that it be grown whenever it can be obtained and wherever there is the slightest chance of room being made for it. To contrast it with a non-weeping conifer of a different colour and of more majestic upper-layer stature is to allow it to give of its best.*

Shades of Green

Green – that colour we find so restful – is, in reality, an extremely broad palette of shades. Somehow, because it is so intrinsically a colour of Nature, it becomes unpleasant when applied to man-made objects, to the extent that it has acquired connotations of bad luck. Whatever may be the truth of that, a green motor car never looks good unless it is bottle-green, like the deep green of older British racing cars. It never seems possible for park seats to be painted anything but the most poisonous shade of green, even when there are so many lovely shades around them from which to copy.

It is seldom that a plant wears a shade of green that is unpleasant. Green is made up of blue and yellow, and leaves can have shades that fall anywhere within the range that this mixture provides, so that there are blue-greens and yellow-greens and greens which can really only be described as 'mid'. The amounts of dark pigmentation determine whether a green is light or dark, whether it be in the blue, yellow, or mid ranges.

Mid-greens

Among the mid-greens are most of the trees that might be thought of as tending towards amorphousness. This is not necessarily so, and it is as well to look for some quality in the foliage of a mid-green tree that reduces the risk of its being seen merely as mediocre.

Birches are almost all of a very ordinary sort of mid-green, and yet their presence is guaranteed to grace any garden. They are not trees on the grand scale like the big oaks, but their height is, in many species, quite enough to qualify them for membership in the upper layer. It is their structure that saves them from mediocrity, while the lack of density in their foliage makes them ideal partners for trees that are more dense, such as the Killarney strawberry tree. To plant a birch with a large-leaved tree only serves to make it look tatty –

Betula papyrifera *has small, attractive, mid-green leaves, but the chief glory of this tree is its bark, an ornament in the Warm and Cold alike.*

almost as if it needed a shave – but set near a holly its lacy foliage will be nicely set off and if it is of a species with beautiful bark and twigs it will look very well in the Cold, too.

Most such birches belong to the middle layer, but one or two are tall. *Betula ermanii* has a pinkish trunk and burnt-orange branches and glossy leaves, while the paperbark birch, *B. papyrifera*, is well known for its white, papery bark. *Betula luminifera* has the largest leaves of any birch, up to 13cm/5in across. Prettily pink as they unfold in spring, these glossy leaves turn a good shade of yellow in autumn.

In the mid-green range individuality becomes an important characteristic – something notably different about the tree's shape, or a way that its leaves work in the mass, will make up for an absence of outstanding colour. The European beech becomes a very large tree indeed – so much so that only the largest gardens can accommodate even one specimen. Furthermore, its roots tend to spread outwards near to the surface and to rob the ground of food and moisture. It is, too, of a rather 'ordinary' green, and it is only its imposing stature at maturity that recommends it. Most young plants are sold for beech hedges – much enjoyed by many people because they keep their browned leaves all winter, but hated by others who think they look merely untidy.

On the other hand, there is a form of the European beech which is not nearly as massive and which is highly ornamental, even though it retains the same shade of plebeian green. This is the fern-leaved beech, whose leaves are either long and thin or pinnately lobed, like small fern-fronds. It tends to develop a tear-drop shape, and has a lightness of presence that makes it show up well

A composition in shades of green. Drama is created by the sharply contrasting shapes of the components and styles of foliage, while harmony reigns through the quiet subtlety of the colour tones. The strongly vertical dark green of Chamaecyparis lawsoniana *'Olbrichii' rises above the powerful, many-leafleted mid-green foliage of* Mahonia × media *'Buckland'. The background is made up of another kind of pinnate foliage, this time more slender and greyish-green.* Fraxinus angustifolia *is a fast-growing, large tree.*

when seen against trees of a heavier make-up. The name we should correctly use for this is *Fagus sylvatica* 'Asplenifolia', although it will often appear in catalogues as *F.s* var. *heterophylla. F.s.* 'Laciniata' is quite different, with leaves rather like those of an oak in which each lobe has been frayed and tattered into threads. This is rare and liable to revert and is hardly a good garden tree anyway. The trouble is that its name is sometimes given to the fern-leaved tree, so you should examine your specimen before buying it to make sure that it is fern leaves that you are getting.

The Dawyck beech, *F.s.* 'Dawyck', is becoming more easily obtainable. This is a strongly fastigiate tree, making a tall column that is far superior in quality to the Lombardy poplar. It is much less likely than the poplar to drop its foliage prematurely and colours up well in autumn to a fine gold. This unusual tree is at its best when seen as an accent among other green trees, where its strongly disciplined line will bring order to other, less well-defined shapes. It is a pity that it is generally planted unimaginatively in rows lining streets or drives. *F.s.* 'Zlatia' is a slow-growing beech which would be the one to choose for the upper layer in smaller gardens. Although it is of an ordinary green once the leaves have matured, its leaves are light yellow in spring and early summer. It is by no means a golden tree, but plain green is needed in the garden and here the colour of the young foliage is a bonus.

Zelkovas are very beech-like, although they are more closely related to elms. *Z. carpinifolia* is often called the Russian elm, but there is less danger of its succumbing to the disease which has destroyed so many true elms. In this species, quite ordinary, mid-green foliage is borne by a tree whose main role is played, leafless, in the Cold, when its multiple trunks, arising from a common ancestor at just 1.5 or 1.8m/5 or 6ft from the ground, form an unmistakable piece of arboreal architecture. Of all garden trees, this is the one which most appeals to children as a climbing tree, and it will not have become too large for any but really small gardens by the time it is big enough to be climbed. *Zelkova serrata* eventually makes a very large tree in some places, but is usually of medium size. Again, it is of medium green, but its dense foliage, consisting of attractive, toothed leaves, gives it that quality of difference that one is searching for.

The zelkovas and the cut-leaved beech are among several other trees which make ideal vehicles for climbers such as *Clematis* and *Wisteria*. The upper layer is not a place where there will be much flower colour, as large trees tend to have insignificant flowers. Wisteria, draping its long racemes of lilac, white, or purple among the lower branches of trees that are not too densely leaved, provides a major element of surprise, and clematis can be chosen to provide flowers over a long period without having to be pruned at all. They are best used among trees of ordinary green, although they are not out of place elsewhere, as their own leaves tend to be of much the same shade and do not show up untidily when out of flower. For this reason, an ash is probably the best host of all for wisterias. There are a few varieties of ash that have unusual characteristics but, with the exception of the weeping ash, whose role in the middle layer can be dramatic, they are either of little value or are extremely rare. The species of ash, when well-grown, are fine trees for large gardens. They do not cast too dense a shade, neither do they rob nearby plants of nourishment. Festooned with wisterias, whose foliage is almost indistinguishable from their own, they are truly magnificent in the spring.

Blue greens

Both the European and the American ashes have mid-green upper sides to their leaves, while the lower surfaces are more silvery. This has led some writers to describe them as being of a blue-green tone, but deceptively so, as they merely (but attractively) appear slightly silvery when the wind blows. Blue tints in foliage are not just silver – they are truly blue, although mixed with green to a greater or a lesser extent. Grey-green is blue-green with the addition of white. The white may appear as a result of hairs on the surfaces of leaves, from thick, waxy skins, or from powdery blooms produced by the leaves. The underlying green will always be on the blue side, never the yellow, and dull, mid-greens which are decorated with white hairs appear merely white, or of a grizzled nature

OPPOSITE Fraxinus ornus, *the manna ash, in flower. While its foliage may be said to be 'merely' mid-green, its lightweight, pinnate leaves lend it distinction and grace. The branch structure of this specimen is particularly good and shows that care was taken with its shaping in its early years.*

ABOVE *Forms of the blue Atlas cedar,* Cedrus atlantica *var.* glauca, *are strongly blue-green. They make beautiful specimens architecturally and their texture and cooling colour contribute considerably to a garden's atmosphere.*

which could never be termed a true grey-green.

The blue Atlas cedar, *Cedrus atlantica* var. *glauca*, is perhaps the best-known of all trees with a blue cast. Although it will be a middle-layer tree for many years, it should not be forgotten that it is a large tree whose wide, flattened top will eventually dominate the upper layer as almost nothing else can. It can be found in most garden centres, and it is tragic to envisage the numbers of such specimens that will end their days having been cut down before maturity. It is sometimes to be seen, most sadly of all, nervously awaiting its imminent fate on a rockery. Care, too, should be taken in seeing that the specimen you are about to buy is truly a blue one. It is not that anyone will have tried to defraud you, merely that it varies from seed from a good, very blue green to the plain green of the species.

Blue foliage positively demands that blue should be found nearby to complement it, but there are traps for the unwary. A large blue Atlas cedar will not be helped if *Picea pungens* 'Koster' is grown close by. It will only call attention to its small size, and the pairing will seem inappropriate. *P.p.* var. *glauca*, on the other hand, allowed to grow to its considerable size at maturity, would be perfect if, and only if, it were a sufficient distance away. This is an example of an extremely strong, dominant statement made by a plant that brooks no contradiction. Anything that is also coniferous and blue will, if it is too small, appear to be a parody. If it is large enough, it must keep a respectful distance.

By contrast, inhabitants of the lowest level may pay homage without appearing out of kilter. Blue agapanthus, irises, *Lithospermum* 'Heavenly Blue', and such things as *Omphalodes luciliae*, whose foliage is blue-green and whose flowers are blue, will echo the blueness of their large neighbour without attempting cheekily to emulate it.

Those who can grow *Eucalyptus* species are far more numerous than they know. Until quite recently, it was thought of as a genus that could be grown only in California or Cornwall, or wherever the winters were almost frost-free. The advent of seed from trees that grow in the hardiest part of their range as far as their native climate is concerned has changed all that, as has the desire on the part of gardeners to experiment with eucalypts. There are now about a dozen species that can be considered by gardeners whose winters involve them in temperatures down to -15°C/5°F and below, even when a wind-chill factor is present. These amazing trees have foliage that is truly distinct and a quite astonishing capacity for fast growth and for rapid regeneration when damaged.

Their uniqueness as a genus makes them a perfect leaven for the daily bread of deciduous and evergreen trees that we are so used to. Their sickle-shaped leaves are arranged so that they receive the minimum of incident sunlight and thus cast the minimum of shade. In addition, they have a juvenile phase, during which smaller, rounded leaves predominate, and they are all more or less

ABOVE *Who could resist the combination of blue-green foliage and snowy white bark that so many of the eucalypts present us with? There are species for all but the coldest gardens and they ask for little but sun and shelter from frosty winds.*

RIGHT Chamaecyparis lawsoniana *'Pembury Blue' is almost truly blue in its foliage colour. Its position here against a taller, dark green background is ideal.*

blue-green. Some of the hardy species are upper-layer trees for the largest gardens. *Eucalyptus gunnii*, the cider gum, is perhaps the hardiest of all and makes a big tree in a relatively short period of time. *E. coccifera*, with smaller, slimmer leaves and a fawn trunk whose smoothness is broken by great bundles and swags of papery, peeled bark, is a magnificent sight, especially in an open space among tall trees with dense, preferably dark green foliage. Nothing can inject an exotic note into a garden quite as definitely as these large eucalypts, although smaller ones are pretty efficient as well.

Among all the taller trees that we may look at for the upper layer in the larger garden, eucalypts are the most amenable to being scaled down. No owner of a small garden need keep them out as being too big, as they can be cut down to whatever size is required – even to ground level – and started again. Indeed, for the lover of unusual foliage, this is a good thing to do, as it will be the rounded, juvenile leaves that will appear. In fact, the largest of all can be grown as bushes, as they will regenerate from the bases and form thickets of stems, all bearing juvenile leaves. Smaller species are perfect middle-layer material or will act as members of the upper layer in small gardens. *E. cypellocarpa*, one of the bluest, does not become a very large tree, and it can be cut back to provide a mass of blue foliage or grown on to make a handsome, medium-sized, patterned-barked tree.

The stems and trunks of most eucalypts (but not all – the ironbarks such as *E. nicholii* have rugged, fissured trunks) are extremely beautiful. They range from pure white to cream, sometimes with blue-green patches, and occasionally with squiggles and other patterns. That such trees should also be evergreen seems almost too much of a good thing; that they flower as well is something which we tend to forget in our preoccupation with their other good qualities. It is no good trying to grow those with red or yellow flowers in cool temperate places. The trees that bear them are all too tender. The hardy ones all have white flowers which consist of brush-like bundles of stamens and they do not clash with anything.

Eucalypts are extremely easy to grow from seed (it is the only way in which they can be grown) and

they grow very quickly – up to 2.75m/9ft a year. It is no great tragedy if you lose one in a very hard winter, as its replacement can be on station in just a few years. Any effort it might take is worth while if our gardens are to be graced by the magnificent foliage of these strange, but lovely trees. It is most important that the full effect of something as dramatic as a eucalypt should not be lost, and for this reason it should be planted with its relationships to other plants in mind. If its leaves can be seen only when silhouetted against the sky, then the blueness is lost, so it should be sited against a background of green. One exotic accent may well appear alien, so it should be answered by another, such as the large leaves of a catalpa at its own level, or by bamboos, yuccas, or other, smaller eucalypts lower down. The flowers of *Callistemon* species – the bottlebrushes – strike the right note and so, oddly, do the spiny thickets of *Colletia armata*. Try to avoid the combination of *Eucalyptus* and *Rhododendron*. It works occasionally in the largest gardens but is usually a mis-match.

Generally speaking, blue-green foliage is found among plants of lesser stature than the taller trees, but there are several large conifers, besides the Atlas cedar, which are definitely blue-green, and some that appear silvery-blue. The Spanish fir, *Abies pinsapo*, has a form called 'Glauca' in which the foliage is blue-grey (although, as with all such foliage colours, there is still a green element). This is a medium to large tree which will grow on thin alkaline soils, and it is saved from the overpowering darkness that is the undoing of so many firs. It is a long-lived tree and hardy to -26°C/-15 °F.

Apart from such conifers with a strongly blue cast, it is worth remembering that most conifers that are green are of a tone that is on the blue side of green. There are not many on the yellow side that are not actually yellow or gold. *Chamaecyparis lawsoniana* is rather variable, but its best forms have a definite waxy glaucousness which incline its green even further towards blue. It is a large tree, whose branches droop and form a more or less narrow cone. This is one of the tall trees that interlocks the foliage layers, as its fans reach down almost to ground level. It is an excellent accent tree, best planted in a group of three if space allows, where its pointed outline can be made to balance more rounded outlines nearby. The form *C.l.* 'Intertexta' has branches which are more spread out – and thus less liable to damage by snow, and the terminal sprays of foliage are large, thick and widely spaced. The distinctive appearance of this tree is most striking, and it is of a definite blue-green.

The bluest variety is *C.l.* 'Pembury Blue'. It will take many years to join the upper level in a large garden, but in medium-sized and smaller gardens it can dominate as a perfectly cone-shaped tree of a colour that comes close to being truly blue. Its background should be the darkest possible – holly, or a dark-leaved evergreen oak are ideal – and at its feet it is best complemented by groupings of smaller, more rounded conifers of light green or golden shades. The cedar of Lebanon, *Cedrus libani*, is, of course, a long-term proposition. It is nowhere near as blue as its cousin the blue Atlas cedar, but its green is on the blue side. Both these trees are most easily recognised in their final, mature forms, when they have attained the typical flat-topped, tiered shape that comes with age; until then they are conical. They thus play two parts in the foliage picture, in the first part of their lives providing vertical features which link the foliage layers.

To allow climbers to flower on conifers might be thought to be out of keeping, as conifers do not have flowers in the way that we understand them – bepetalled and colourful. Strangely enough, though, it works. *Clematis montana* is a regular traffic-stopper on a busy road near where I live; it grows up into a tall specimen of Irish yew and looks like a springtime Christmas tree. The really tall conical conifers and the columnar ones look wonderful at midsummer when they play host to such vigorously climbing roses as 'Rambling Rector', whose clusters of white flowers make the trees look as though they have been decked out for a wedding. It is the unexpected impact of the flowers that makes them so delightful, and they are only unexpected if the foliage of the climbing plants is small and not too noticeable. Those who would think it a good idea to have a major foliage contrast here, such as a large-leaved vine, should forget it. The result is merely untidy and makes one want to pull the offending plant away.

Pinus wallichiana *has long-needled foliage that resembles the brushes of old-fashioned chimney-sweeps. This Himalayan species is markedly blue-green and grows to be a large tree. If it is not crowded it will be furnished with its lovely needles right down to ground level and will form a strong linking motif between the three layers. It is hardy, but will not grow on shallow limestone soils.*

Several pines are on the blue side of green. The Scots pine, *Pinus sylvestris*, like so many conifer species, is openly conical when young and fairly quick-growing on good soils. At maturity it is one of the noblest and most beautiful of trees, developing a pinkish-tawny bark on its higher branches and bearing a fine head of foliage above a long, straight bole. Few coniferous trees lend quite the air of distinction that the Scots pine does to mixed plantings of trees, but its main drawback is that its beauty will eventually be made ugly by the dead snags of cast branches. Investment in a half-day's work by a good tree surgeon will remedy this, however, and nobody who has seen it, perfectly at home among broad-leaved trees, could ever deny it a place in a large garden. This pine is bone hardy, and so is the Korean pine, *Pinus koraiensis*. This is on a smaller scale but is, if anything, bluer. Once again conical in youth, it has an openly branched habit at adulthood. It needs a climate with warm summers to give of its best, and for that reason makes better specimens in the United States than in Britain.

Any pine is an asset in the garden. The stiff, unyielding way in which they stand up to wind when everything else may be thrashing about creates a contrast all of its own, and nothing can compare with them for foliage which is so totally different from everything else in appearance and behaviour. *Pinus muricata* and *P. radiata* are both Californian and are the Bishop and the Monterey pines respectively. The Bishop pine is the better proposition, as it is very hardy, notwithstanding its birthplace. Both hold their cones unopened for up to forty years, so that cones may be seen on old branches and are in such numbers that they become an intrinsic part of the essential natures of the trees when seen in silhouette. They are both fast-growing and can easily reach 30m/100ft in height in seventy years. These two extraordinary pines share with others the property of somehow lending to the garden an air of durability and distinction that is hard to pin down but is nevertheless very real.

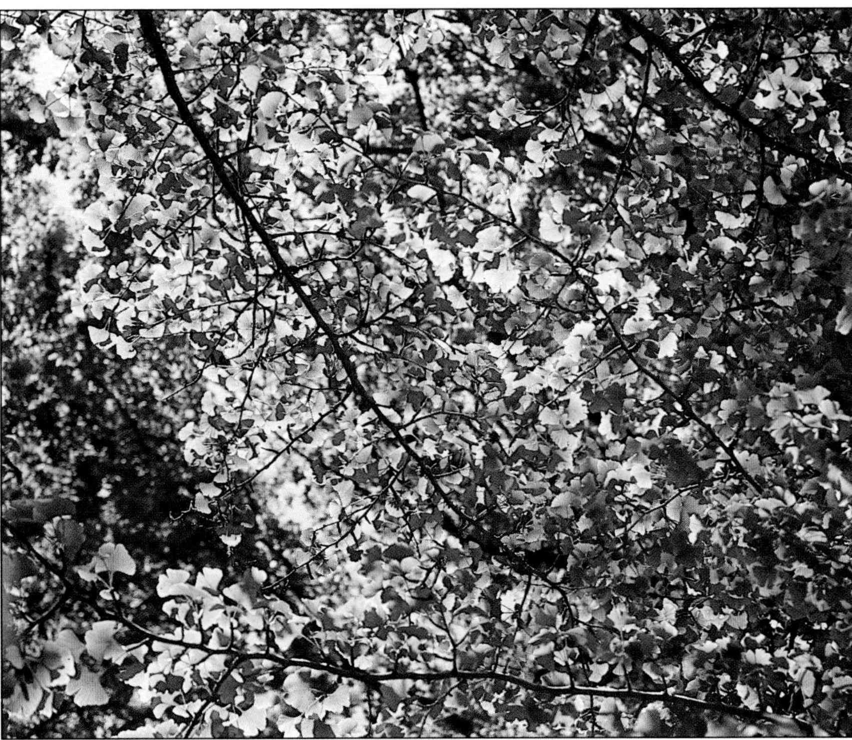

The yellowness in leaves that are yellow-green is brought out strongly by the sun's rays. Many oaks appear golden against the sun, as does this Chinese Maidenhair tree, Ginkgo biloba.

Yellow greens

Trees whose leaves are on the yellow side of green are neither as easily detectable nor as common as those whose green veers towards blue. Blue-greens may be accentuated by waxes and blooms, but these are absent when green is tinged with yellow. Yellow-green foliage is different from that which is frankly yellow or gold, although the difference is a matter of degree. What we may regard as yellow-green is foliage which in certain lights looks mid-green while in others has a definite yellow cast.

This is best illustrated by examples. The English oak, *Quercus robur*, has leaves which in the height of summer appear to be a dull green, which then becomes duller and greyer as the season progresses. The new leaves in spring are of a definite golden hue, but this soon passes, and gold only appears again in the autumn. However, when the sun shines through the leaves of this oak, no matter that it is late in summer, they appear to be of the brightest gold. No mere mid-green tree can do this, and it is certainly beyond the capacity of any blue-green tree. This quality is shared by the Maidenhair tree, *Ginkgo biloba*, whose autumn colour is of the purest yellow, and whose quite light green leaves display an innate yellowness when the sun is behind them.

Many deciduous oaks are yellow-green, and it is this quality that allows them to appear fresh and cheerful even when each leaf may have become soiled and grimy after a long summer. The deciduous oaks are the perfect trees under which shrubs may be grown without their soil being robbed. There is no better group of trees for providing the dappled shade that rhododendrons and other shallow-rooted shrubs require, and their leaves break down quickly to provide a highly nutritious leaf-mould. Both European and American oaks are ideal for these purposes, as are some of the Asiatic ones.

The American red oak, *Q. rubra*, is a tree with large, conspicuous, deeply-lobed leaves which turn to red or a mixture of red and yellow in autumn. It is a perfect shade tree for large-leaved rho-

A young specimen of Ginkgo biloba *shows brilliant golden colour. Trees whose summer foliage is on the yellow side of green tend to turn gold in autumn; the pigments that give green a blue cast are liable to form red autumn tones.*

dodendrons, whose simple, stiffer leaves contrast well with the much more mobile, differently-shaped leaves of the oak. It is, however, a lime-hater, and although this does not affect its association with rhododendrons, it limits its general use in gardens. The same applies to *Q. coccinea*, the scarlet oak, so-called because of its autumn colouring. This is very variable, however, and the species is usually available as the variety 'Splendens', a form with unusually brilliant and reliable autumn colours that is propagated by grafting. Where this can be grown – which is to say where space and the soil allow – it should be very near the top of the list of the most desirable of the larger trees.

It is most encouraging that in an age when it might be thought that the planting of large trees is declining in our mobile societies, and in which the 'small' garden is constantly on the lips of those who speak through the various gardening media, there is a greatly increased interest in oaks of all kinds, including the large, deciduous ones. Perhaps the speed of growth associated with the Hungarian oak, *Q. frainetto*, increases its appeal. It is certainly fast-growing, on any type of soil. For whatever reason it is becoming a popular tree, those who plant it will not be disappointed, as its fine, neat shape, straight habit and attractive bark are all excellent qualities. It is as a foliage tree, though, that it scores the very top marks: its large leaves, often exceeding 20cm/8in in length, are neatly and regularly lobed and of a very pleasing green which is just on the yellow side.

Q. canariensis, the Algerian oak (the discrepancy between the Latin and the vernacular names is a quirk of the palaeobotanists) is similar, although rather more dense. It is a large-leaved tree, whose distinction lies in its keeping its leaves until the very depths of winter. This is a quality shared only by *Q. × turneri*, a very rare, medium-sized oak, but one which cheats – it is a hybrid with an evergreen oak. Perhaps the most elegant of all the deciduous oaks is the pin oak, *Q. palustris*. It grows quite quickly and resembles the scarlet oak, although its deeply-lobed leaves are smaller. It is more reliable in producing its scarlet autumn colour and is very attractive indeed as a young tree. If the choice came down to just two deciduous oaks that would eventually grow large, but which would play a significant part in the garden as they grew, then this and *Q. frainetto* would be hard to beat.

Any oak, once planted, must not be moved. Once its roots have started to invade the area around the original ball of soil, it is a fixture and will die if interfered with. The care with which an oak's position is chosen must, therefore, be meticulous and its ultimate height and spread catered for even if they are far in the future. A few specialist nurseries will supply really young plants, and growing them from acorns is simple if they are sown shortly after collection in the autumn. No oak will tolerate being stored until the spring, as the water content of acorns is critical. The white oaks, which are mainly European and Asian, will germinate straight away, while the mainly American black oaks will wait until the spring.

For a tall, slender tree, *Ginkgo biloba* is unmatched. Its leaves are on the yellow side of green and are like those of no other tree. Each one is

The foliage of Ginkgo biloba *strikes a distinctive note. Its leaves are fan-shaped, and some trees have a tabulate branch structure almost like that of a cornus.*

shaped like an upside-down ace of spades, its veins radiating outwards from where the leaf blade meets its long stalk. It is a living fossil, neither a conifer nor a broad-leaved tree but antedating both, and at one time was thought to have been extinct for millions of years. Its position should be in front of other trees, where its dramatic shape and its way of being clothed in branches almost to ground level can be set off. It will link the layers of foliage, especially in the autumn, when it is of the purest, brightest light gold for much longer than most trees. Gardens do not have to be large to accomodate it, as it has little spread and it is not a soil-robber, nor is it an underminer of structures. This is one tree, however, upon which it would be inappropriate to grow climbers. Although its extraordinary foliage can be set off against normal broadleaves or coniferous trees, the intimate contact between flowers and a tree which developed long before flowers seems out of place.

Generally speaking, large trees do not present us with the problem of reconciling compatible types of foliage with possibly incompatible flowers, because nearly all of them have flowers that are insignificant, especially when they occur far above the ground. One large tree with yellow-green leaves does have interesting flowers, however; it is the tulip tree, *Liriodendron tulipifera*. Even so, its blooms are more curious than ornamental. They are tulip shaped, but are of a greenish yellow that makes them easy to miss, especially as they are not produced on young trees. It is the foliage of this tree that is its main attraction. Each leaf is quite large – about 15cm/6in long and half as wide – and has three lobes. The side lobes at the base are sharply pointed, but the middle one is much larger and looks as though its top has been cut off using an inwardly-curved guillotine.

Such unusual foliage, borne by a tree with open structure and a rounded head, is wasted among such things as oaks, especially American ones whose leaves are also strongly lobed. It is a good companion for tall conifers or for anything that has dark, dense foliage which will effect a complete contrast. Never lean anything against a tulip tree. Its bark is readily injured and a great many mature ones can be seen with large wounds a metre or so above the ground. Oddly enough, a severely damaged liriodendron will, when cut to ground level, regenerate from strong shoots and make one of the best displays of foliage that one could wish. Large, lush leaves with beautiful golden autumn colour will arise, driven by the intact root system. It is no part of my brief to advocate the cutting down of trees, but it is a fact that tulip trees are brittle and can become a nuisance when grown large. If you find an old one in your new garden and there is a strong case for its removal, it is worth remembering that its stump may be kept to some purpose.

One of the largest trees is a poplar, *Populus × canadensis* 'Serotina'. This widely-planted tree has a shape like a long-stemmed goblet. Its leaves are mid-green with pale undersides and it is unusual in that it remains leafless until the late spring. 'Serotina Aurea' is quite different. Its shape is more rounded, and its young leaves – also appearing very late – are pure yellow. They become yellow again in autumn, but during the summer they are of a bright yellow-green. This is not a tree which you would wish to advertise too strongly in the Cold, as it is pretty ordinary when out of leaf, but a background of dark, evergreen foliage will hide its gauntness while showing off its colour in the Warm. This is not a 'golden' tree – but it is the ultimate in the expression of the yellow component of green.

Dark greens

Trees with dark green foliage are all too often written off as being sombre. They are thought of as depressing, heavy, and cheerless, especially in climates where springs and summers may have many days when the skies are grey. There is some truth in this, as an unrelieved plantation of dark

The tulip tree, Liriodendron tulipifera, *has intriguing flowers that highlight the unique shape of its yellow-green leaves. This tree will grow to be very large, and will clothe itself in foliage from top to bottom.*

green is all these things. However, rather like a jeweller's shop in which cases full of nothing but green velvet cushions would be very boring, dark green foliage serves beautifully to show off the brighter wares that the garden has to offer.

There are two kinds of dark green found in foliage. One is a colour that is blacker than mid-green but is still immediately recognisable as green – it is not so black as to fall within the olive-green range. Such trees as *Liquidambar, Aesculus* and many magnolias come into this group. The other is so dark that its greenness quite disappears in certain lights and, even when well-lit, is definitely olive-green. Many of the trees that fall into this latter group are evergreen, and are among the most valuable subjects for using as our jeweller's cushions.

Evergreen broadleaf trees become less of a possibility the colder your climate, and the more you have to rely on conifers for evergreen foliage. Nevertheless, it has to get really cold before they are ruled out altogether, and the milder parts of cool temperate zones can support quite a wide population of broadleaf evergreens.

Quercus ilex is probably the hardiest of the evergreen oaks. It will stand severe frosts with windchill, but will not tolerate them for more than a few days at a time. It is, where the climate suits it, a large, bushy, densely-leaved tree of the blackest olive green, and it makes a first-class windbreak. What is more, it can be clipped to make an extremely strong hedge which will keep the strongest winds out of the garden, even if they be salt-laden. As a tall tree for the upper layer it is superb, with a great, billowing head through which it is impossible to see. Good trees which have not been drawn up by over-close planting are clothed with foliage to within a metre or so of the ground and are marvellous backgrounds against which brighter neighbours can be shown to their best advantage, whether they are in the upper layer as well or lower down. All the other shades of green stand out beautifully against a dark backcloth such as this, and nothing other than the darkest greens will show off blues and blue-greens quite as well.

The Lucombe oak is rather greyer and not as dark. It is a hybrid between the Turkey oak,

FAR LEFT *The holm oak,* Quercus ilex, *displaying its dark green foliage. It is a European 'live', or evergreen, oak of massive weight and stature which is an upper layer member* par excellence *when mature, and imposing enough even as it grows. In gardens that are not too cold it acts as a shelter against winds and as a broad backdrop for lighter foliage tones.*

CENTRE LEFT *The evocation of a wintry cheerfulness is inescapable in hollies that berry as freely as* Ilex aquifolium *'Pyramidalis'. This cultivar combines glossy, dark green, nearly spineless foliage with a most engaging shape.*

LEFT *Sometimes the roles of the differing shades of green can be reversed. Here the dark green of a form of* Cryptomeria japonica, *the Japanese 'cedar', abandons its usual role as a backdrop for bluer or lighter foliage and helps by its prominence to draw particular attention to itself as well as to the blue-green conifer beyond.*

Q. cerris and the cork oak, *Q. suber*. Neither is hardy in cold areas, but each is almost on a par with *Q. ilex* – the Turkey oak is probably even hardier and has transmitted this quality through to the hybrid. The Lucombe is a stately tree, much larger in cultivation than the cork oak, and it is a valuable addition to the rather limited repertoire of evergreen broad-leaved trees. The main practical drawback with evergreen oaks is that their leaves fall at midsummer as the new ones emerge, so that they are at their untidiest just when you want the garden looking its best. What is more, they take forever to break down into leaf mould.

It would be a mistake to think that hollies cannot be part of the upper layer of foliage in large gardens. *Ilex aquifolium*, the common holly, can make a tree of 25m/80ft and often attains 18.5m/60ft. It is not a realistic proposition for gardeners to start from scratch with the aim of growing such a large tree; it is much better to regard it as a middle-layer member, but those who have larger gardens may well have inherited very large hollies. Whether it is grown as a plant for the middle layer, either as a hedge or as a specimen, or found as a large tree, nothing makes a finer foil for other plants, whether it is their foliage, flowers or both that one wants to display. Its berries (if it is female) are, of course, a welcome midwinter bonus.

Among dark green conifers, several are fast-growing and make large trees with branches that sweep to within a short distance of the ground. *Thuja plicata*, the western red cedar, is not a cedar at all, but is the source of the timber that is given

Acer pseudoplatanus *'Prinz Handjery', whose shrimp-like tones are displayed to great effect against a dark background. Truly dark, almost sombre greens gain stature when associated with such bright shades.*

the name. It is a first-class windbreak which, like the evergreen oak, can be clipped to make a large, impenetrable hedge. As a free-growing tree it needs plenty of room, and this needs to be borne in mind if it is to be planted as a 'viewing screen' behind light green, blue, and golden conifers – a job which it carries out to perfection. The flattened sprays of thuja foliage are very different from the densely-packed, stiletto-shaped leaves of *Cryptomeria japonica*. This, too, is referred to as a cedar without actually being one at all. Again, it is fast-growing, hardy and, like the thuja, will do well on almost all soils. These two, with *Chamaecyparis lawsoniana* to provide blue-green between the dark green trees, would be enough to make a dark backdrop of foliage for more colourful foliage as well as an effective screen against wind. The garden would have to be large – 1000sqm/quarter of an acre at least – but could be a cold garden, as all three trees are hardy.

Backed by these trees, such things as *Robinia pseudoacacia* 'Frisia' would really shine, their gold intensified by the darkness behind. The large leaves of a well-grown *Magnolia* × *soulangiana* would be a great contrast with the small, densely packed leaves of the conifers and would have visual value when the goblet-shaped, white, purple-stained flowers had been and gone. *Acer palmatum* 'Atropurpureum' would have both the shape and colour of its wine-purple foliage highlighted strongly, and its autumn flame-red would blaze like a beacon against the dark greens and blue-green.

In your imagination, take away the background conifers to reveal the sky beyond. The robinia's gold becomes less solid, while the magnolia foliage looks merely heavy alongside it. The acer appears blackly in silhouette and, as all three are deciduous, all the Cold provides you with is some undistinguished bare branches. That the maple will by now have been wind-blasted is another matter; at best there would be no sign of its autumn colour. Which is the more cheerful picture? The one in which the sombre dark greens highlight the brightness and interest of the foreground, or that which shows the sky but prevents the plants from displaying their true worth? Surely the former, with its use of what many people think of as dull and depressing trees and too big at that.

That dark green that does not become as black as the deeper, olive greens is found largely among deciduous trees. *Liquidambar styraciflua* is one of the most beautiful of trees, and its lobed leaves often lead it to being mistaken for a maple. Indeed, its autumn colour is just as dramatic – a deep crimson that starts very early. There is a form called 'Lane Roberts' whose colour is even richer in autumn but any specimen of this species will need a good, deep, loamy soil to give of its best. *Aesculus indica*, so much finer and lighter in structure than the common horse chestnut, has leaves that come within the dark shades of green. Their characteristically palmate leaves lend yet another shape to those among large trees that have leaves that can be distinguished individually from below. Here, at last, is a large tree with conspicūous flowers; its pink blossoms in upright trusses turn it magically into a giant candelabrum. Both these deciduous trees are very hardy, and a garden that contained them and the three conifers would be well on the way to having an imposing upper layer of foliage, in spite of the fact that all of its greens were at the dark end of the spectrum.

Light greens

There are not many large trees whose foliage is light green (as opposed to yellow-green). Luckily, several of them have large leaves as well, so they fulfil a dual purpose.

Populus lasiocarpa is unaccountably uncommon in gardens. It has bright, light green leaves up to 30cm/12in long and 20cm/8in wide and is one of the best of all trees for foliage. As a contrast to dense, dark foliage it is superb, its heart-shaped leaves with bright red stalks looking like those of only two other trees – the catalpas and *Idesia polycarpa*. Why it is not seen more often is a mystery, as it can be propagated with consummate ease by sticking branches in the ground in autumn. It is not a particularly large tree, but is certainly an upper-layer tree for all but the largest gardens. The leaves of *Catalpa bignonioides* are similar. This is the Indian bean tree – not from India at all, but from the eastern United States – and it, too, is not disposed to grow all that tall. It is, however, one of the most striking of trees when in flower. The blooms are like foxgloves, white with purple and yellow spots, and they are borne in late summer, an excellent quality in a tree. The 'beans' are just that – long, dark brown pods full of seeds.

Idesia polycarpa, like its brethren with large, heart-shaped leaves, is not very tall, but is a big enough tree for the upper layer of most gardens. Its light green leaves, like those of *Populus lasiocarpa*, have red leaf-stalks. This Japanese tree used to be uncommon, but is becoming far less so as more and more seed is being made available, from which it germinates freely if sown in spring. A poplar that ought to be seen more often is *P. wilsonii*, which is similar to *P. lasiocarpa*. Its leaves are not quite so large, but are nonetheless most imposing, and they are of a light green which has a touch of blue in it. The branchlets have a decidedly blue-purple cast and this feature and their sturdiness makes *P. wilsonii* an ornament in the Cold.

RIGHT A light, fresh green is characteristic of the foliage of Catalpa bignonioides, *a tree with large leaves and a broad habit. Its upright inflorescences contrast well with the flatness of its leaves.*

LEFT The origin of the London plane is not certain, but some think it to be a form of Platanus orientalis, *the Oriental plane. Its foliage is light mid-green and capable of feats of brilliance under the influence of sunshine. Take care, however, that it is not exposed to too much pollution lest its lovely colour becomes dulled.*

Populus nigra is the species to which the Lombardy poplar belongs, but the type is not at all pencil-like, but rugged and heavily-branched. Its foliage is light green (although a trifle dirty-looking), but it is a tree of which to be wary because its roots are notoriously wide-ranging and liable to seek out the nearest drain and throttle it. Perhaps the most magnificent light green tree is the Oriental plane. This is a tree of very large size and of great longevity. Its widely-spreading branches and its big, deeply five-lobed leaves lend it a majesty that is maintained throughout the year – even in the Cold it is worth travelling to see. Again, it is uncommon in gardens, but that is no good reason for failing to mention a tree whose foliage is second to none. It is, however, not a species that one would use as a foil for other things; it demands isolation and admiration for itself alone, otherwise it tends to get jealous and to hide its fine features.

Catalpa bignonioides *'Aurea' is the golden form of the Indian bean tree. Light greens develop golden forms more readily than dark greens, although gold variegation will be found in the latter.*

PURPLES

The range of tones that the word 'purple' is applied to in speaking of leaves is really nothing of the sort. It is a group of colours that vary from bright copper to a dark mixture in which copper is enriched by an infusion of blue-black. Unfortunately, a distinction is made between copper and purple which is understood by horticulturists, so, as it does not usually pay to fight against convention, it will be as well to stick to the term 'purple' for the blue-copper shades.

The copper beech is probably the best-known tree that has foliage within this range. Indeed it is in itself a range of clones which vary from very light, almost orangey copper to quite a dark purple. The names are confusing, and trees can be found called *Fagus sylvatica* var. *purpurea* or under several cultivar names such as 'Riversii'. It is well worth looking out for 'Rohanii', as it is that pearl beyond price, a purple form of the cut-leaved beech. Seedlings of copper beeches are sometimes offered, and they can vary from almost green to deep 'purple'. Many people find that trees with only a light copper tone are the most attractive, and they are certainly most delightful when planted so that the afternoon sun shines obliquely through the leaves, making a brilliant display of gold and copper. Foliage in the deeper shades cannot achieve this magical effect.

Some eminent plantsmen detest copper and purple foliage with a passion that others find a little hard to understand. There is no doubt that it is a disaster if it is overdone, like anything else, but the use of purple is one of the most effective ploys in gardening with foliage. Because it stands out so strongly, it is extremely useful for linking parts of the garden together, or for establishing relationships between plants set at a distance from one another. Done too often, the message is destroyed and the garden takes on an unattractive, speckled or diffuse appearance. Used in moderation, however, it is often a stunning addition to a garden of any size.

Purple in the upper layer can be achieved relatively quickly using a form of the Norway maple, *Acer platanoides*, called 'Crimson King' – yet another complication in the description of

RIGHT *The leaves of the copper or purple beech,* Fagus sylvatica *var.* purpurea. *Deeply coloured forms, as well as those with lighter, more coppery tints, make striking and effective statements.*

BELOW *The genuinely purple leaves of* Acer platanoides *'Crimson King'. This should be sited with the greatest care, as its colour is strong and heavy.*

'purple'; it is not crimson at all, but deep blue-copper. My own taste lies rather towards the lighter copper shades, but this is indeed a remarkable and striking tree which should, perhaps, be the sole representative of its colour type in even the largest gardens at the upper layer level. The perfect counterpart at the middle level is *Cotinus coggygria* 'Velvet Cloak', a newly raised shrub of just as deep a colour and which also needs to be planted with a light hand. *Cotinus* 'Grace' is much lighter, with a hint of green in its brownish-red leaves. It can take two or three years to establish itself, but after a tremulous beginning takes off like a rocket.

The ordinary sycamore is a dreadful nuisance in gardens because of its habit of seeding itself everywhere with considerable stealth. Deep-rooted seedlings seem to arrive as if by magic, always in the worst possible places. *Acer pseudoplatanus* 'Atropurpureum' – sometimes labelled as 'Spaethii' – is a form that is well-behaved in this respect. The upper surfaces of the leaves are of the usual undistinguished muddy green, but the undersides are a colour that really does come somewhere near what you and I understand as purple. It is a tree of fast growth that can become deformed if it is not given enough room, but a well-grown specimen can be a subtle addition to the leafy canopy, as the purple only shows itself when the leaves are blown by the wind.

GOLDS

Gold is a colour of which much is made in catalogues but which is quite rare. Many cultivars of trees and shrubs with names like 'Golden King', 'Gold Spire', and so on are really yellow-green, or are truly golden for only a short time in the year. Furthermore, because yellow foliage is less charged with chlorophyll, golden – or yellow – forms of large trees tend to be slow-growing, sometimes very much so. *Quercus robur* 'Concordia', for example, might at first be thought of with delight as a golden version of the mighty English oak, but in fact is extremely slow-growing and makes a somewhat stunted (though not unattractive) tree.

To inject any 'gold' at all into the upper layer of

large trees we must look to conifers, and there are not so many of them, either. Lawson cypress provides us with one or two good ones, such as 'Lane' (Lanei), which makes a tall column of rather whippy, feathery foliage which is golden all year round. 'Lutea' is somewhat sturdier and has downswept branches that are resistant to damage by snow. It is also of a good, lasting colour; the two go well together because the character of each is quite different. They, and anything else that is gold, look at their best when displayed against a blue-green background, and nothing could be better for this than 'Triomf van Boskoop', which is one of the largest forms of Lawson cypress and is of a lovely, fresh blue-green. Indeed in spring it is almost blue.

Cupressus macrocarpa, possibly because it has 'California' stamped on its birth certificate, has an undeserved reputation for tenderness. It is an extremely large tree, of a dark mid-green, which is columnar for many years before becoming cedar-shaped. Two of its offspring, 'Lutea' and 'Donard Gold', are spoken of as golden varieties, but they are both yellow-green. 'Lutea' is more so, and it turns almost true green as the summer matures. 'Donard Gold' has more soundly-based pretensions to goldenness and is a very fine tree indeed. Even if it is yellow-green, its colour is deep and rich and it will be a great asset to the middle layer of foliage for many years before promoting itself into the higher ranks.

Chamaecyparis, to which Lawson cypress belongs, and *Cupressus* are closely related but there are pitfalls if you treat them alike. *Chamaecyparis* needs a good, deep soil that does not dry out, while *Cupressus* will tolerate almost any soil except a wet one. *Chamaecyparis* species and cultivars can be moved easily while they are still young, while this is death to *Cupressus*. Moreover, × *Cupressocyparis leylandii*, that ubiquitous hedging conifer, which is a hybrid between species of both genera, can be clipped without turning a hair. To clip *Cupressus macrocarpa* is to sentence it to death. It is worth noting, too, that *Cupressus macrocarpa* is a very large tree indeed, and it has passed this quality on to its hybrid offspring enhanced by hybrid vigour. 'Leylandii' is the fastest-growing evergreen tree of all, apart from a eucalypt or two, so it is well worth considering as an imposing, cedar-like tree with foliage in the mid-green range. Just don't let your hedge get out of hand!

Gold is an excellent 'sandwich' colour. We have discussed how dark backgrounds help to set off bright features, but light colours can play this role in reverse. Where the two effects are combined as a 'sandwich', golden foliage is used to its own best advantage as well as that of its neighbours. Staying with conifers for a moment, and recalling the two golden forms of Lawson cypress growing against the blue-green background of 'Triomf van Boskoop', would it not complete the group to have the narrow, pencil-like blue-green columns of *Juniperus virginiana* 'Skyrocket' outlined against the more bulky cypresses? The reinforcement of vertical accents such as this is not to overdo them. 'Skyrocket' is the slimmest of conifers and as such is almost always recommended as a vertical accent in an otherwise horizontal picture. It usually looks fairly silly in such positions – more of an excrescence than an ornament – and is much better seen against a vertical golden background than sticking up in the air all alone.

Gold occurs as a variegation in one or two large trees, but is effective only when they are young. By the time a tree has become large, the variegation is at too far a distance for the eye to discern and the overall effect is one of yellow-green. *Liriodendron tulipifera* 'Aureomarginatum' is excellent in its early days, and is probably best grown as a stooled plant after a few years so that its large, brightly margined leaves can contribute a splash of brightness to the middle layer. Left to itself, it will run up for the light and become nondescript, and you will need binoculars to pick out its pattern.

The weeping golden beech, *Fagus sylvatica* 'Aurea Pendula', has been known since the end of the last century but is not often seen. This is a pity, as it is a tall, elegant tree which contributes to the foliage scene by its shape as well as its colour. Its leaves are gold in their youth, but soon become yellow-green and, what is more, burn in the sun which might be thought to prolong their early colour. It is better off in shade but, of course, this makes the brief splash of gold pass even more quickly.

A neatly related planting in which colour is used to great advantage. The Robinia pseudoacacia *'Frisia' finds itself felicitously planted next to the tall, golden conifer, which links the layers together and carries the gold motif from the upper layer (borrowed from the robinia) down to its feet, at ground level. Yellow and orange flowers in the foreground, along with low-growing yellow-leaved or variegated shrubs, complete a well-integrated colour grouping.*

THE · MIDDLE · LAYER

SMALLER TREES & SHRUBS

When you enter a garden that is new to you, your first impressions are influenced by the largest plants, whose size and colour attract your initial attention and contribute most to a garden's 'mood'. But it is the trees and shrubs at eye level that firmly define the character of a garden. While the upper layer establishes the garden's size and whether it is light or dark, sheltered or exposed, what the middle layer of foliage tells you is specific. Is the garden fussy or well-ordered? Is the standard of cultivation good or bad? Are the plants happy or somewhat neglected? And while all three layers play their parts in engendering the feelings that you have about the garden as a whole, your eye still focuses most readily on the middle layer of foliage; it attracts close attention and is therefore best discussed not in terms of colour but of leaf shape and size.

It must not be forgotten that many of the larger trees from the upper layer have foliage that extends down into the middle one, if not right down to ground level. Indeed, it is a poorly designed garden in which this does not happen, for then the interlocking effect between layers is lost, along with the vertical composition of the garden picture. The detail at eye level that makes us aware of the characteristics of leaves leads us to notice and study more closely the individual leaves of upper-layer trees. A leaf which, 25m/80ft or so above our heads, is merely part of the greenery can, on intimate acquaintance, take on the cloak of drama.

The middle layer, then, will be filled with the leaves of trees and shrubs of all but the smallest sizes. Climbers will be seen there too, as will the foliage of the largest perennials, both herbaceous and evergreen. Every kind of leaf imaginable will congregate where the eye falls most readily, and in this horticultural examination-room the gardener will be tested thoroughly on his knowledge and use of the shapes and sizes of leaves.

Leaves come in such a diversity of shapes that it is by no means easy to classify them into neat, convenient groups. That is Nature for you, however, and some effort has to be made, otherwise we shall all become confused. Luckily it is possible to make two broad divisions: simple and compound leaves.

COMPOUND FOLIAGE

A compound leaf is made up of separate subsidiary leaflets. The most basic form is trifoliolate, which means 'three-leafleted'. This word is often confused with trifoliate, which means 'three-leaved'. And just to add to the difficulty, there are trifoliolate plants among whose leaves are some with more than three leaflets.

All compound leaves have an air of weightlessness about them, even the biggest, dark green ones. *Choisya ternata* is a good example of this type of leaf. Compared with the rather stodgy laurel, the leaves of the choisya have a lightness that makes the orange-blossom-scented, white flowers seem to float on airy waves of deep green;

At eye level, subtlety in variegation is evident. The gold in the leaf of Eleagnus pungens *'Maculata' contrasts with the yellow margins of* Ilex × altaclarensis *'Golden King'.*

they are quite small, too, so the last thing they want is to be overpowered by their own foliage. *Choisya ternata* does not mind whether it is in sun or in shade and it flowers for a long period in late spring and early summer. It is a good companion for rhododendrons, whose conditions it enjoys, especially as it will flower after they have finished. Its foliage, too, makes a pretty contrast with their simple leaves, and is equally evergreen. Unlike the rhododendrons, though, it does not hate lime, and can be grown to advantage on a limy soil with skimmias, set off against the gold of *Weigela* 'Looymansii Aurea', or used to put a bit of flower power among some of the smaller hollies.

Acer negundo, the box elder, grows quickly to make a good tree for the middle level of a large garden or the upper level of a smaller one. Its trifoliolate leaves cast only a light shade, in which much play can be made with contrasting shapes – the pinnate fronds of ferns, the large, hazel-like leaves of *Fothergilla monticola,* a small shrub that is buttery yellow in autumn, and the various carpet textures of geraniums, *Tellima grandiflora,* and massed cyclamen. It is a maple, not an elder at all, and it is deciduous. In the Cold it is nothing very much, but its variety *violaceum* has purple shoots that are eye-catching. *Acer negundo* itself occasionally has leaves with more than three leaflets; the purple-stemmed form usually has five to start with.

The hardy climber *Sinofranchetia chinensis* is telling as a foliage plant, with leaves consisting of three large leaflets – up to 15cm/6in long on 23cm/9in stalks. The foliage is glaucous as well as being bold and unusually shaped. A host with contrasting foliage is essential; it looks well growing in a tree of *Robinia pseudoacacia* (but not 'Frisia'), or in anything with light green, small entire, or finely pinnate leaves.

Prince of all trifoliolate trees of the middle layer (or the upper in small gardens) is the Moroccan broom, *Cytisus battandieri.* I have a weakness for truly silver leaves and I return again and again to this superb botanical aristocrat. Among its many virtues is a fine leaf shape. It is worth mentioning in passing that it grows perfectly well from seed, which is set abundantly in good summers, and there is no excuse for the iniquitous practice, so common in the trade, of grafting it on to laburnum, another trifoliolate plant that can send up huge suckers as soon as your back is turned. The leaflets are of the same size as the broom and are not all that easily spotted, so do try to buy it on its own roots. Laburnum itself is a dull thing, a classic case of a plant whose foliage should be attractive but is not. It falls into the middest of mid-greens and has a permanently dirty look. It flowers for a short time and then its poison, common to every part of it, permeates its seeds and pods, setting a deadly trap for any child who may take them for peas. Unfortunately, the leaflets are an attractive, shiny, light silvery green at first, which is why they can hide among those of *Cytisus battandieri.* To purchase the one grafted on the other is to introduce a vegetable cuckoo into your garden.

Choisya ternata, *often called Mexican orange blossom, is one of the many shrubs that are a great deal hardier than might be supposed, and it will tolerate freezing temperatures for quite lengthy periods. Its long-lasting, scented flowers find their perfect accompaniment in the brightly glossy, deep green trifoliolate leaves, which are themselves aromatic.*

Much smaller, light green trifoliolate leaves, clustered tightly along the entire length of each branch and branchlet, characterise *Adenocarpus foliolosus*. This Canary Island endemic is so lovely that, although its use is restricted to gardens that have only slight frosts, it is a shrub to be sought after at all costs for the cool greenhouse or conservatory. It is the nearest thing to a plant wearing a green woolly jumper that I have ever seen, and it produces its brilliant yellow pea-flowers all the year round, setting enough seed to furnish every glasshouse in the world with its enchanting presence.

The most fragrant flowers of any hardy tree – and it is a tree, although not a large one – are to be found on the American hop tree, *Ptelea trifoliata.* Its three-leafleted leaves are aromatic, as are the fruits, which have been put forward as a substitute for true hops. Its charms are not sufficiently appreciated and it should be grown far more widely. It is hardy, easily propagated from cuttings (the seed is rarely good), and would make a fine lawn specimen in many a small garden, scenting the air around a favourite sitting-out spot.

Cytisus battandieri *is called the pineapple broom because of the scent of its flowers, which is said to resemble pineapple – although some think it is more like banana, or even lemon. The three-leafleted form of the silvery leaves can clearly be seen here.*

Digitate leaves

In digitate leaves the leaflets (usually five, but sometimes more) radiate from a single point. One of the best known of all plants with digitate leaves is the true Virginia creeper, *Parthenocissus quinquefolia.* It is seen far less often than it was many years ago, as it has to a very large extent been supplanted by the Japanese *P. tricuspidata,* a species which has three different kinds of leaves. They can be more or less simple and entire, simple and deeply three-lobed, or compound with three leaflets. The true Virginia creeper, a much less coarse and more elegant plant, has digitate leaves with five leaflets. Both these climbers are renowned for their brilliant autumn colour and for the speed with which they cover walls or buildings. They are not, unfortunately, as often seen growing up trees. A Virginia creeper, red as dawn in the autumn, is a magnificent sight when seen clothing the trunk of a Scots pine, with the topmost branches of the pine emerging, tawny pink, from its embrace.

Both species climb without support, as they have sucker-pads on their tendrils. *P. inserta,* also sold as Virginia creeper, has none, and so needs artificial support and is no good for growing into trees. *P. tricuspidata* becomes coarse just where you least want it to be – at eye level in the middle layer – so let a plea go out for a return of the previously popular *P. quinquefolia.*

The horse chestnuts have digitate leaves, but these are large trees and more suitable for the upper layers of large gardens. For the middle layer, the buckeyes, which are smaller relations of the horse chestnuts, are supreme. The species most often seen is *Aesculus parviflora,* and with good reason. It is very much like a shrubby horse chestnut, not much more than 3.6m/12ft high, and its leaves are large, with 23cm/9in leaflets. What makes them of elegant appearance is the long taper from the broadest parts of the leaflets down to the points of origin. This wide-open look makes for great lightness in what is a large leaf. This is yet another example of a leaf of which one speaks in terms of largeness but for which the word 'bold' is inappropriate. The flower spikes are glorious 30cm/12in long upright candles of white with pink or red anthers, appearing in late summer when colour among woody plants is at such a premium. The autumn colour is clear yellow and comes early, so that flowering and autumn colouring follow closely upon one another. It is superb among lacecap hydrangeas, with whose flowers its own will not clash, presenting instead upright inflorescences among the almost-open, flat flowers of its neighbours.

Members of the Dissectum group of *Acer palmatum* (the cut-leaved Japanese maples) have leaves with five, seven or nine leaflets, that are best thought of as digitate. Many of these maples are foliage plants of the first rank for the middle layer. Of course, they are slow-growing and will inhabit the lowest level for some time, but it is among the eye-level trees and shrubs that they will spend most of their lives.

There always seem to be new varieties of Japanese maples arriving in general cultivation, but I shall concentrate here on two varieties of long-standing reputation. It is these that I would choose for a garden of quality (where gimmickry and freakishness have no place).

Acer palmatum 'Dissectum' is often sold as 'Dissectum Viride' – no matter; it is the green one. Its leaves are a bright, light green, marvellous reflected in water or seen against the bright colours of azaleas in the spring. *A.p.* 'Dissectum Atropurpureum' has leaves of deep 'purple' – actually a rich, deep copper. Its autumn colour is magnificent when the plant is in good condition. However, condition is something of a problem with Japanese maples. They are sadly susceptible to the burning effects of the sun, the desiccation of wind, and to the cutting-back that a late spring frost can cause.

Pinnate leaves

By far the largest class of compound leaves is the pinnate. These are leaves that are shaped like feathers – each leaf has a long, central stalk, the *rachis*, along which rows of leaflets are dispersed, usually – but not always – opposite one another. This leaf form, seen on most palms and many ferns, is of great value in the garden: pinnate leaves cast only light shade, and their very featheriness leavens the foliage scene and brings buoyancy to places where sombreness might otherwise creep in. Looked at from beneath, the leaves break up light and, particularly when the sun is overhead, diffuse its rays into iridescent fractions. There is a gossamer air about the play of light on pinnate foliage.

RIGHT The digitate form of the leaves of Parthenocissus quinquefolia, *the true Virginia creeper, is almost as attractive a feature as the superb autumn colour. Because each leaflet moves independently the effect is always light.*

OPPOSITE The finely cut leaves of this Japanese maple have a filigree appearance that is especially attractive when it is allied to breathtaking autumn colour.

BELOW The digitate leaves of the cut-leaved Japanese maple react to every passing breeze.

The lightest leaves of all are double pinnate. Here the rachis, instead of sporting rows of pinnae, gives rise to subsidiary ranks of pinnate leaflets. Sometimes the whole leaves can be counted among the largest in cultivation, and yet their presence lends softness and levity, in complete contrast to similarly large non-pinnate leaves which tend to impose oppression or gloom, suggesting the steamy jungle or the dripping forest.

Where the climate is kind, and where there is an established overhead canopy of deciduous trees that do not rob the ground, an Australian tree fern (not from New Zealand as many suppose) is an exemplar of all that is most magical in bi-pinnate leaves. *Dicksonia antarctica* is a true fern, so it should be deemed to have fronds, not leaves, but for gardening purposes they are the ultimate in twice-pinnate structures, each whole frond being up to 90cm/36in wide and more than twice as long, made up of tiny 2.5 by 1.5cm/1 by ½in divisions. To look up through them is a wonderful experience. It is to be transported back to the days when dinosaurs strode the earth – or at the very least it is hard to think of the twentieth century when such primitive but utterly beautiful plants turn their magic upon you. The moist, mild, rhododendron-ridden gardens in which this hardiest tree fern will grow are scarce, but the spell of the bi-pinnate can be woven even in much colder gardens – not in quite the same awe-inspiring way, but to good effect.

In all but the coldest of temperate gardens, *Aralia elata*, the Japanese angelica tree, can be grown. This rarely reaches 9m/30ft and is much more commonly seen at about 4.5m/15ft, while its leaves are usually 90cm/36in long by 60cm/24in wide, or even a quarter as large again. These are large leaves by any standards and yet the expression 'bold' cannot apply because of the delicate, lacy tracery made by the arching sprays of 5cm/2in leaflets in soft, light green (on the yellow side). What a foil this is for stiff, immobile, solid, dark-green leaves! Plant it among camellias, skimmias, or smaller rhododendrons, or let it parasol over shrub roses – but keep it away from plants that are redolent of the hot and the dry.

The aralia's flowering is spectacular and well-timed: summer's end sees enormous panicles of

small white flowers which hang below the leaves, collectively looking like an enormous lace Elizabethan ruff. The variegated forms, both in gold and cream, can be obtained grafted on to the species, but such is the rarity of suitable scions that the prices of these plants are high indeed. They can also succumb to extra-severe winters, arising from the stocks as the pure, plain-leaved species. Winter damage is reduced in poor soils, but at the expense of some opulence. Rich soils will induce a softness in a plant which is already pithy, so a balance must be struck. Shelter from wind and excellent drainage are probably the best recipe.

The Australian acacias – the mimosas of florists – are too tender for all but the mildest gardens, but are without peer as trees for the conservatory. In the open garden they occupy the middle layer – in some species within a year or two – and the bi-pinnate species lend blue-green tones and the ultimate in featheriness – *Acacia dealbata*, for example, could almost be said to have plumage rather than foliage, and its myriad yellow pompoms are a miracle under glass in the depths of winter or outside just a little later.

Far hardier is *Albizia julibrissin*. This has mimosa-like foliage but is deciduous, whereas the *Acacia* version is evergreen. The pink flower-heads are more like bottle brushes than pompoms and the pinker the flowers, the more the plant seems to be from a hardier provenance. Korean forms are pinker and hardier than the Chinese and Afghan ones, and there has recently been introduced a form with red flowers that is hardier still. I have found that the plants I have grown from seed during the past ten years share the flower colour and hardiness of those I have bought full-grown during the same period. They are all of a definite, deep pink, and have stood up to winter temperatures with deep wind-chill factors that I would not have dreamed it possible for them to survive. This is a species most certainly to associate with plants from hot, dry regions, and the blue flowers and entire leaves of the summer-flowering *Ceanothus* species or varieties in the Delinianus group of the genus benefit from the contrast with its pink flowers and bi-pinnate leaves.

Koelreuteria paniculata, more euphonically called the golden rain tree, is not obviously

OPPOSITE *The tree fern,* Dicksonia antarctica, *can be grown out of doors in gardens where frosts are neither common nor severe. Its delicate fronds lend a mysterious quality to the garden.*

RIGHT *The foliage of a mature specimen of* Aralia elata *'Variegata' is stunningly beautiful, especially when the creamy-white margins of the leaves are complemented by the clouds of white flowers.*

BELOW Rosa rubrifolia *is so light and natural in appearance that it looks quite at home in most situations. Here, it graces an old stone wall.*

bi-pinnate, but if you look more closely at its quite large leaves – they can be as much as 46cm/18in long – you will see that they are so, in as much as the primary leaflets begin to break up progressively from the base of the leaf until, about two-thirds of the way to the end, they have separated into individual secondary leaflets arranged, rather unusually, opposite one another. Here is another small to medium-sized tree with a long period of summer interest. Golden flowers in late summer, valuable enough in their own right, are followed by golden autumn foliage.

I have said already that it is a mistake to put all one's eggs in the autumn basket when looking for foliage colour. *Gleditsia triacanthos* 'Sunburst' is golden-leaved in the spring and becomes greener as the season progresses. At midsummer, its colour is such a refreshing mixture of green and yellow that seeing it on a hot day, waving its frond-like leaves at the edge of a lawn and giving light shade to some of the smaller shrubs, is the optical equivalent of a cool drink of lime juice. It is bi-pinnate only in part, most of its 30cm/12in long leaves being merely pinnate, but is possessed of all the lightness that one would expect from finely divided leaves. It is a good upper-layer tree for small gardens, and for those of recent foundation, but it belongs firmly in the middle layer of the larger garden, where it should be sited so that it is not over-shaded, lest it lose its gold.

The Kentucky coffee tree, *Gymnocladus dioica*, will not do well in shade at all. Although it is a large tree in its native eastern and central United States, it is usually small in cultivation, and thus fits into the middle foliage layer. It is among the most beautiful of hardy trees for foliage, with bi-pinnate leaves 90cm/36in long and 60cm/24in wide, but it is one of the least attractive in the Cold, when its leaves have fallen to reveal an ugly, sparse branch structure.

Singly-pinnate leaves do not have the frond-like delicacy and ultra-lightness of those that are bi-pinnate, but they are still feathery and leavening. One has only to compare woodland of oak with stands of mixed oak and ash to see how the pinnate leaves of the ash lighten the whole canopy. These are large trees, though, with atmosphere as their domain. The lightening effects of compound

The pinnate leaves of Gleditsia triacanthos *'Sunburst' are as refined in colour as they are in shape, their golden yellow tinged with a soft lime green.*

leaves on character are the business of the middle layer.

Does one really *look* at the foliage of some plants? Or is one's attention always drawn to those famous 'foliage' plants of which so much is made? When did you last think about the leaves of a species rose and how they are made up? They are pinnate, often with nine or more leaflets, and their disposition on arching branches makes them as light and airy as many other more obvious 'foliage' plants.

The use of foliage in the garden should not be restricted to the obvious, but should include plants that repay closer study. *Rosa rubrifolia,* for instance, is a shrub of retiring habits which appeals little to 'foliage' people and yet it is supremely beautiful. An aristocractic framework of curving branches bears leaves of seven leaflets or so whose colour suggests that a blue-grey leaflet has been dipped lingeringly in the finest burgundy. Its flowers are a rich pink and the hips that follow are long-lasting, large, and bright red. It is a quiet celebration of planthood that does not pall in the Cold when there are no leaves to adorn the bristles, whiskers, needles and hooks that clothe the stems. We are told that we must now call it *R. glauca* – not a bad name – but the tangles over its name are as thorny as the plant. My advice is to stick to the 'old' name for now, at least.

It is not possible to do more than hint at the possibilities for the use of rose foliage. I grow *R. rubrifolia* quite near a path, in one place with *Azara microphylla* 'Variegata', a rare, slow-growing shrub that is so difficult to propagate that it is virtually never offered, but one whose masses of tiny, gold-variegated leaves provide an ideal contrast. In another spot I have planted it against a plain background of grass. This latter siting is more effective. A myriad of combinations must be possible with all the shrub and species roses, including the climbers – and yet they are almost universally ignored.

When next you consider planting roses, try some of the old-fashioned ones, but place them in a mixed border so that the greyish compound leaves of the albas have their greyness picked out by artemisias, and the small, dark green leaflets of the chinas contrast with the large, pleated leaves of *Hosta sieboldiana.* The small flowers will not look out of place when the hostas send up their lilac-tinted white spikes, either.

The elders are a ubiquitous group of plants. Members of the genus *Sambucus* strongly resemble one another, so that someone familiar with the flora of the central Floridian forest would immediately recognise the British native species, and vice versa. The berries, flat-headed flowers and, of course, pinnate foliage are common to all of them. Only some forms are useful in gardens however, and only one species is grown for its flowers and berries as well as for its foliage. Mostly it is leaf shape and colour that makes the genus truly garden-worthy.

Sambucus nigra 'Aurea' is a first-class yellow-leaved shrub. There is a hint of lime in the yellow – a sort of acid edge – that calls for careful placement or even for isolating it as a specimen, lest its neighbours look pallid by comparison. *S.n.* 'Marginata' is liked by some, but to my eye appears dull and its colours remind me of the cream-and-green much beloved by those unimaginative individuals who decree the colour schemes for the corridors of government institutions. *S.n.* 'Laciniata' is the cut-leaved elder. It is quite a hard plant to like and has not got the presence that *S. racemosa* 'Plumosa' has. The leaflets of this better plant have teeth set so deep that the leaves seem almost bi-pinnate. *S.r.* 'Plumosa Aurea' is one of the best of all golden-leaved deciduous shrubs, and is first class in every way. *Sambucus racemosa* flowers in the spring; its very large panicles of red berries ripen in summer. The golden form, replete with bright fruits, is one of the finest sights in all gardening if it is well grown, well displayed and if there is a bit of luck about. This is a plant that will either flower and berry like mad or sulk and refuse to perform, often for no obvious reason. However, it often seems to do well planted against a warm wall with its roots in shade. And the golden leaves are perfectly set off by almost any kind of wall, be it stone or brick.

A similar situation is enjoyed by the pinnate-leaved *Sorbaria aitchisonii*. Many shrubs and trees with pinnate leaves are late-summer flowering, and this is no exception. Its large panicles of white flowers are frothy confections among the many-leafleted leaves, as if the wind had picked up the delicate foam from a bubble-bath and left fairy-light sprinklings of it on the plant. It is a mistake always to contrast complete opposites. There is a temptation to place simple-leaved plants with compound ones, and one might expect to see *Sorbaria aitchisonii* growing behind something like *Berberis*. Not a bad idea: there is, too, the evergreen nature of the berberis to counter the deciduousness of the sorbaria. But it would be just as effective to display two kinds of pinnate foliage, one of which is evergreen. *Mahonia*, a close relative of *Berberis*, would do very well.

LEFT *The golden-leaved elder* Sambucus racemosa *'Plumosa Aurea' is superb as a foliage accent.*

BELOW Mahonia japonica, *with its evergreen pinnate foliage, is one of the noblest of all garden shrubs. Its lax racemes of scented flowers, borne during the winter, give rise to luxurious clusters of blue-bloomed berries.*

Mahonia aquifolium, the Oregon grape, is not the species that would fit the bill in this sort of situation. It is a denizen of the lower level and not tall enough to accompany shrubs of the middle layer. *M. japonica*, though, is one of the noblest of all plants in its foliage and is of just the right size. The leaves are between 30 and 60cm/12 and 24in long and have thirteen to nineteen stiff, spine-tipped, shiny, dark green leaflets. The whole plant is a series of whorls of these leaves so that, although its habit is upright, the overall effect is of horizontal strata. Its long, pendulous racemes of lemon-yellow, scented flowers are a major feature of the garden in winter. The upright racemes of *M. bealei* are less subtle and far too geometric, looking like a stack of chimney sweep's brushes of assorted lengths. The lax, laid-back ones of *M. japonica* add an insouciance that is truly elegant.

These mahonias are hardy, but there are others which need just that little promise of milder winters. *M. lomariifolia* has longer leaves with more and smaller leaflets, and it has been hybridised to create *M.* × *media*, among whose cultivars are 'Charity' and 'Winter Sun'. They are fine plants with foliage that is truly bold, easy to praise, with the following reservations: the trace of tenderness makes them suspect for general planting; they tend towards legginess and have inherited the upright flower-heads of *M. lomariifolia* instead of the sophisticated ones of their other parent, *M. japonica*. Mahonias will grow on most soils, including very limy ones. Oddly enough, on a lime-free soil they look as if they truly belong with the rhododendrons, pieris and azaleas that surround them. Then again, put them among the viburnums, osmanthuses and spiraeas on lime and they seem equally at home. It is hard to misplace a mahonia, even though its structure is so uncompromising. Perhaps that is the answer – it immediately dominates its neighbours and imposes on them the fitness of its position.

Evergreen leaves that are pinnate are a rarity among woody plants until the subtropical flora is reached, and it is trees and shrubs that make up the bulk of the middle layer in all but the smallest gardens. Many ferns are pinnate, or bi-pinnate, but only the tender tree ferns grow to the required size; even *Osmunda regalis* is not quite tall enough to qualify. There are pinnate-leaved climbers, of course, but few of them are evergreen. One – and it is only possible to grow it outside in mild gardens – is the lobster claw, *Clianthus puniceus*, from New Zealand. This is one of the best of all wall plants where it can be grown. Its foliage is a repeated zig-zag of herringbone patterns in the richest apple-green, and it has a pleasing habit of flattening itself against the wall, displaying its leaves to the full. In spring conspicuous clusters of big flowers, each like that of a giant pea and coloured a red that any Buckingham Palace guardsman might envy for his coat, decorate the

Wisterias, like other pinnate-leaved climbers, can appear at once opulent and graceful.

plant like ornaments on a Christmas tree. It is superb in a conservatory among the little yellow powder-puffs of acacias, if your garden is too cold for it.

The hardier pinnate climbers are deciduous. Wisterias, so celebrated for their hanging racemes of flowers, are not appreciated enough for their foliage, which consists of large leaves with many leaflets. The best way to display wisterias is to grow them into trees, where they will need little pruning and will flower well, decorating the trees as if with an extra flowering. In gardens where you want to make walls and pergolas into foliage features, these plants have few equals, with their 30cm/12in long leaves tending to hang just where they are best. There are two species commonly in cultivation – *W. sinensis* and *W. floribunda*. As far as foliage effect goes, there is not much to choose between them. Both have leaves of about the same length, but *W. floribunda* has more leaflets and is, therefore, the lighter and more suited for gardens on the smaller side. Both are, however, extremely rapid and robust growers and need a lot of pruning when grown against a wall or pergola. To keep them in bounds, they can be pruned in the winter, heading them back to the size desired. For flower production, though, the whippy side-shoots should be reduced to two buds in the middle of the summer. This will not affect their foliage at all.

The nomenclature can be confusing. *W. sinensis* should never be bought unless it carries a varietal name, because unscrupulous nurseries have flooded the market with inferior seedlings. *W. floribunda* is often sold with the cultivar name 'Macrobotrys'. This is, in fact, a group name for several cultivars, some of which have pink flowers, others lilac and double and still others making racemes of up to 90cm/36in long. These last are supposed to be 'Macrobotrys' but are in fact 'Multijuga' – a very old name which was once used for the species. With all this confusion you could end up with a wisteria that you do not want, so tell the nursery what colour flowers and what length of raceme you are after and bother about the name afterwards.

The trumpet vine, *Campsis radicans,* conjures up a picture of large scarlet and orange flowers flaming from a wall in late summer and early autumn. Quite right, too, but who mentions the fact that it has pinnate leaves of well over 30cm/12in long with up to eleven leaflets? It is one of the self-clinging climbers like ivy, and needs the warmth of a wall, although it is hardy almost everywhere. It is from the south-eastern states of the U.S., and is yet another extraordinary incidence of the likeness between the flora of eastern America and eastern Asia in its closeness to the Chinese species, *C. grandiflora.* The two, when hybridised, gave rise to *C.* × *tagliabuana,* of which the finest form is 'Madame Galen'. This has bigger flowers in much larger clusters, like its Chinese parent, but has retained the downy undersides of the leaves from its American one.

Rhus typhina, the stag's horn sumach, must be rated highly in any catalogue of foliage plants. Its long pinnate leaves and young shoots are covered with russet-brown hairs like the 'velvet' on the horns of a male deer. In autumn they take on magnificent orange-red, yellow and purple colours. There is also a beautiful, cut-leafleted form, whose correct name is *R.t.* 'Dissecta', which is delightfully feathery and whose autumn colours are unsurpassed.

You can grow *Rhus typhina* anywhere, even in the poorest soil, and it is perfectly hardy. Should you want really large, luxuriant foliage, it can be cut back nearly to ground level each spring and fed liberally with well-rotted manure. Growths up to man-height will ensue, bearing leaves as long as 90cm/36in with conspicuous 'velvet' and autumn colour.

Seed is often available of a smallish tree called *Phellodendron amurense.* This has handsome pinnate leaves which in young trees are very large and striking at just the right point in the middle layer. It is supposed to develop a corky bark – hence its name of Amur cork tree – and to have abundant clusters of small white flowers at midsummer over which the bees hover feverishly. You may germinate this seed at home and quickly have a sapling on your hands that is very fetching indeed. However, it will almost certainly never develop into a tree unless you live where summers are hot, winters are cold, and the seasons do not dicker about before deciding to change. Japanese provenances produce much better results than Amur ones, but they are

OPPOSITE Acer japonicum *'Aureum' is difficult to grow well. Although it is hardy, it requires good drainage and a site away from cold winds. It needs light, or its colour will become greenish rather than yellow, but if there is too much sun the leaves will be scorched. A large specimen in first-class condition is quite a rare sight.*

still not too good. Unfortunately, they get called *P.a.* var. *japonicum,* which is a crying shame, as the species *P. japonicum* is first class in most temperate conditions and develops its nice, corky bark while flowering like mad and causing inebriated bees to totter about in its luxuriant foliage.

Decaisnea fargesii, a member of the Lardizabalaceae family of climbers, is a plant which should be better known. It would make a good addition to so many gardens. A hardy shrub with 90cm/36in long hanging pinnate leaves, it quickly reaches 6m/20ft high and then appears to stop there. The flower panicles are over 30cm/12in long and hang from the ends of the branches rather unexcitingly, but the steel-blue seed pods are decorative. What is more, this is a true 'foliage plant' which enjoys growing in shade, provided that it has a rich soil. Late spring frosts may damage it, but adequate shelter should prevent this in most years.

BELOW The Joseph's-coat autumn colours of Rhus typhina, *the stag's horn sumach, are quite splendid. Most gardeners feel that they amply compensate for this shrub's annoying habit of suckering.*

SIMPLE FOLIAGE

In some simple leaves, it is shape that is the most significant characteristic. Others are better differentiated by size.

Simple lobed leaves

If a lobed leaf has its veins pinnately arranged, it is said to be pinnately lobed. If the veins radiate from one point, it is palmately lobed. This distinction may sound academic, but in fact the shape of a leaf depends to a large extent on how its veins are arranged. Leaves with pinnate lobing tend to be long, while palmate lobing produces leaves of the maple type. Many oaks have pinnately-lobed leaves. These include large trees like the common English and American oaks, which belong in the upper layer, but also some of the small or medium-sized oaks that belong properly in the middle layer.

Quercus macrocarpa, from eastern North America, grows to impressive heights in its native stands but is much smaller in cultivation, especially in maritime climates. Its leaves are always large and conspicuous, however, and can be over 30cm/12in long; they are deeply lobed in the lower half, but almost unlobed in the upper. *Q. aliena* is an oak with similarly large leaves. This small tree is Japanese. Its leaves represent another extreme of oak foliage – in *Q. macrocarpa* the lobes come very close to the midrib; in this species they are little more than large teeth. What the two have in common is a very bright, lettucey freshness to the young leaves and a habit of producing them at odd times during the season, even though both are deciduous. The later leaves are often the largest and quickest growing, and it is interesting and unusual to see two different shades of green on the same tree.

The large oaks with simple lobed leaves often have much larger leaves when they are young than when they are mature. Therefore, they are at their best at the middle-level stage, where they can contribute to the character-forming part of garden foliage. A tree such as *Quercus velutina,* the black oak, whose pinnately-lobed leaves are 30cm/12in or more long at this stage, is not something to put in just for its ultimate effect in the upper layer. While planting large trees may be an investment for the future, like the laying down of port, their efficacy as foliage trees when they are very young may also influence your choice.

There purports to be a variety of *Q. velutina* whose leaves are truly enormous, as long as

46cm/18in. This variety, 'Rubrifolia', if it exists at all, is probably represented by one known tree, and has been extensively confused with *Q.v.* 'Albertsii', whose leaves are as large but whose autumn colours are not so good, nor so red. Young plants of 'Albertsii' have appeared recently in a few nurseries, and their price has every justification in being above rubies. Large-leaved oaks are of truly great value in the garden, although it is a pity that so many of them, like the black oak, will not tolerate lime. Their very fallen leaves make a fascinating carpet of shapes, while when young they are perfect planted with the uniformly even-edged rhododendrons, the spiky lances of bamboos, or, most perfectly of all, calming down the fussiness of smaller, variegated foliage with their comforting green largeness.

Many maples have palmately-lobed leaves. Some of these trees will eventually reach sizes which qualify them for the upper layer, but most will be middle-layer trees for the greater parts of

ABOVE Acer palmatum *'Senkaki' is also known as the coral-bark maple. The leaves turn canary yellow in autumn, then drop to reveal the network of bright red twigs and branches. This tree should always be placed so that the branches can be seen against green, the darker the better.*

their lives. In smaller gardens they will attain senior status at a younger age.

Acer rubrum can be a large tree in its American home, but rarely reaches more than middle height away from it. Its leaves are large – up to 12cm/5in across when grown with plenty of moisture – and are three- or five-lobed, the outside lobes having further subdivisions. It is one of the maples that flowers conspicuously, in this case in large clusters of red that appear before the leaves. With this feature, nice-looking leaves and brilliant autumn colour, what more could one ask? Poise, for one thing, so that it can shine in the Cold. Well, it has it: it is a pleasant structure of ascending branches when leafless. Most forms produce unmatched autumn effects in the United States, but fail to do so in countries with maritime, as opposed to continental, climates. All is by no means lost in this respect, though, as 'October Glory' lives up to its name by covering itself in a mantle of the most vivid furnace-red that any artist's imagination could demand.

A. rufinerve has leaves whose lobing is similar but which are different at the base, so that they have a more heart-shaped appearance. The veins of the leaves are red when young and the autumn colour is a good, bright red, but not as reliably as in *A. rubrum* 'October Glory'. It is one of a group of trees that never reach large sizes in gardens, and which have an additional attractive feature – their bark. These so-called 'snakebark' maples have trunks that are green or reddish striated with white so as to create an impression of snakeskin. They are lovely in the Cold, and should be placed so that each phase of their beauty may be closely appreciated as it succeeds the last.

A. pensylvanicum has perhaps the best bark of all these maples. From an early age the bark is bright green with very white striations, while its markedly lobed and toothed leaves remain large – 15cm/6in or more – throughout its life. The bark becomes russet in older trees, but the butter-gold autumn foliage seems to match it well. It makes an ideal lawn specimen for a garden of any size.

Another American maple which is a good lawn specimen, but this time for the small garden, is *A. circinatum*. The vine maple has, as you might expect, seven- or nine-lobed leaves with heart-shaped, almost circular bases. It also has good flowers in spring, with white-and-maroon blooms appearing before quite large leaves. This is one of the smallest maples and is a first-class shrub when set among plants with plain, even-outlined leaves. To look attractive on the lawn, its lower branches may be removed when it is young so as to furnish it with a short trunk.

The small species of *Acer* which is variously known as *A. villosum*, *A franchetii* or *A. sterculiaceum* has particularly large and striking leaves, 25cm/10in across and mainly three- but often five-lobed. I have them displayed at just above head height with a background of the red-purple foliage of the purple-leaved plum *Prunus*

OPPOSITE RIGHT In continental climates, the large palmate leaves of Acer rubrum *colour gorgeously in autumn.*

BELOW Acer saccharum, *the sugar maple, is seen at its best in continental climates, where the contrast between Warm and Cold is sharp. Generally, the greater the difference between summer heat and winter cold, the more spectacular the autumn colour.*

cerasifera 'Pissardii' (syn. *P.c.* 'Atropurpurea'), and the combination is enchanting.

There are some plants that instantly set a mood; and few are so effective in this as *Fatsia japonica*. Its huge, palmate nine-lobed evergreen leaves (between 30 and 60cm/12 and 24in across) look so jungly it is difficult to believe that, given some shelter from cold winds, *Fatsia* is quite hardy. If you want to bluff the unwary into thinking that the climate of your garden is much milder than it really is, try *Fatsia japonica* with some yuccas and young Chusan palms. The large leaves, with their violently contrasting but strangely complementary shapes, together create the effect of a temperate jungle.

Paulownia tomentosa is another plant – a tree rather than a shrub – whose foliage lends a touch of the exotic. As a tree it is never very large, although it grows quickly for the first few years. Its leaves are made up of three to five shallow lobes, so that they have a characteristically pentagonal shape; they are quite velvety and about 15cm/6in wide or more. The scented flowers are like foxgloves, of a light purple colour (true purple, not the 'purple' of foliage descriptions), and borne in spring before the leaves. Because cold winters destroy the flower buds, which are formed in autumn, the paulownia does not bloom often. Grown with *Decaisnea fargesii* and *Fatsia japonica*, the paulownia's foliage can create an ambience of looming lushness. Generally the best use for it, especially as it can be renewed from seed with the utmost ease, is to grow several and cut them down to ground level every winter. Well fed and watered, each stool will, when its new shoots are reduced to one, send up a stem of up to 2.75m/9ft tall, with huge leaves 90cm/36in across. These are no pinnate confections of lightness but robust, flat plates redolent of dripping, tropical hideaways and of shade from the fierce sun.

It is by using middle-layer foliage like this that its essential character-building nature becomes evident. As we investigate the shapes of leaves, we begin to be aware of the effects of size. Size and shape are not elements that can be considered in isolation; the two together give the middle layer its centre-stage importance. The distinction made between large leaves that are palmately lobed and

LEFT Paulownia tomentosa, *the foxglove tree, is another plant with exotic-looking foliage. Its great aprons of palmately-lobed leaves suggest a tropical rain forest.*

BELOW *The common fig,* Ficus carica, *growing in harmony with the mountain pine,* Pinus mugo *– an inspired juxotoposition of two plants which in Nature are widely contrasted in every way.*

those that are digitately compound is not academic, but is a matter of practical concern. A digitately compound leaf, composed of leaflets which arise from a central point, has much more mobility than one which is merely divided into lobes. Its component parts move independently, while the palmate leaf moves as a whole. For this reason the mood-setting qualities of large, palmately-lobed leaves are of great value. They create the sensation of being in a much warmer climate than exists in a cool-temperate garden. Leaves of such large size, exotic shapes and relative immobility are very rare in plants that can be grown away from sub-tropical or warm-temperate areas.

Ficus carica, the common fig, with its thick-textured, deeply lobed leaves, is another surprisingly hardy plant. It is true that the fruits of the fig are produced in the open only in very mild areas; elsewhere a wall is needed. But if you forget the fruits and grow the fig for its foliage it will stand perfectly well as a tree in the open, enduring even severe frost, although in a really cold place it may sometimes be cut back to ground level. As I write, the only plants visible to me are a stand of ancient figs, some 4.5m/15ft high, growing 45m/150ft or so from the open sea. And yet, whoever heard of figs being used as a maritime windbreak?

Kalopanax, like *Fatsia* a member of the Aralia family, also has palmately-lobed leaves and will stand cold weather. *Kalopanax pictus* grows to be a considerable tree; however, it takes a long time to attain heights over 6m/20ft, so its place can safely be assumed to be in the middle layer. In early life its five- or seven-lobed leaves are more than 30cm/12in wide, becoming rather less than that in older trees. They are shallowly lobed for the most part, although forms can be found in which the leaves are cut as much as three-quarters of the way through instead of the more usual third. They are glossy dark green and contrast strongly with the greyish-white spines and prickles fearsomely arranged along the branches. Try climbing it and see where it gets you!

Just as one never seems to see the fig grown for its foliage, *Kalopanax pictus* never seems to be made the most of. This plant always seems to me to cry out for neighbours that will conspire with it to create an illusion of steamy heat. Planted a short distance from the waterside it could easily and effectively complement the so-called giant rhubarb, *Gunnera manicata*. This herbaceous plant has the largest leaves of any capable of growing in climates where there is considerable winter frost. They can grow anew each season to 2.5m/8ft wide on stems of equal height and are shallowly lobed and covered with spikes and sharp stubble such as might be found on the chin of a Goliath. *Gunnera manicata* is often planted with ornamental forms of true rhubarbs. This is a mistake, as it belittles the *Rheum* species. It requires something of its own kind – a tree with the look of a fellow-denizen of the jungle – and the kalopanax, spines and all, fits the bill perfectly.

Simple linear leaves

That section of the plant kingdom that includes the grasses and a great many bulbs goes in for simple, straight, long leaves in a big way. The section is properly referred to as the monocotyledons, and the leaves as linear. By far the greater number of these plants will be found in the lowest layer of foliage, where snowdrops, scillas and the grasses of the lawns are to be found. But there is a tribe of plants with narrow leaves that are, in their

Gunnera manicata, *the giant rhubarb, has the largest leaves that can be grown in a temperate climate.*

ABOVE *The upright, linear foliage of* Yucca filamentosa *gives rise to some of the stateliest flowers of summer. In this planting the long, curving leaves of the Japanese loquat,* Eriobotrya japonica, *emphasise the suggestion of warmth made by the yucca.*

OPPOSITE Miscanthus sinensis *brings an exotic note to the garden. The combination of straight leaves and arching flower stems is irresistible.*

own way, as exotically important to the middle layer as those with big, jungly leaves.

These narrow, often spine-tipped, leaves are redolent of Mediterranean and warm-temperate climates, where long, hot summers call for the reduction of the leaf surface so as to conserve moisture. Few plants with leaves of this type can be grown where winters are characterised by prolonged periods of cold; many indeed can be attempted only in the softest maritime climates if outside the warmer regions of the world. However, there are some that will succeed over a wide climatic range.

One or two species of *Yucca* – a genus of woody monocotyledons – will tolerate a surprising degree of cold; it is snow that is their enemy. They are natives of the southeastern part of North America and as such are used to severe cold but not to deep, long-lasting snowfalls, which break their stems. *Yucca recurvifolia* is a branched, tree-like plant which can grow quite readily to 1.8m/6ft or more in height. The mid-green leaves are up to 90cm/36in long in a series of rosettes, one to each branch. The large white flowers are arranged in erect, 90cm/36in panicles and are borne in late summer. This plant is a native of Georgia and tolerates light snow very well; it also grows well in much colder climates. Even more surprising is *Y. gloriosa*, which does not turn a hair in temperatures as low as -18°C/0°F for short periods or -15 °C/5°F for days at a time. The surprising part is that it comes from as far south as the Florida panhandle and does not naturally occur further north than South Carolina. It is, with *Y. recurvifolia*, one of the two best species for flowers, but its foliage is much superior, especially in the variegated form, in which cream and grey are added to the green of the stiffly-held clumps of leaves, on stout 1.2m/4ft trunks.

Yucca filamentosa, which is also hardy, belongs properly to the lower layer, since its narrow grey leaves do not grow much taller than 60cm/24in. However, its flowers impinge on the middle layer, as the stems can be up to 1.8m/6ft in height. This yucca flowers freely and a group planting makes the best of its leaves, with their odd, curling filaments along the margins. Its best plant associates are its own kind.

Most yuccas, however, should be planted with other plants that look appropriate in a hot, dry setting. One way of linking them to the rest of the garden is to use clumps of bold grasses, whose stems and leaves are similarly linear, and which go well both with plants that come from dry areas and those from moister places. *Miscanthus sinensis* 'Zebrinus' is perfect for the job. It grows to 1.8m/6ft, and so qualifies as a middle-layer plant in its own right, but needs, as do all grasses, foliage of the strongest personality nearby. Its leaves are green at first, but develop criss-crossing yellow bands in the latter part of the summer, just as the yuccas flower.

Phormium tenax, the New Zealand flax, is a plant that does not revel in hot, dry conditions, and yet it can be grown quite close to yuccas if the tiger grass intervenes – from here it can be associated with totally different plants, and a natural progression will be made from the dry yuccas to the moist flax. Phormiums belong to a class of plants that does not fit into the usual horticultural jargon. They are not shrubs (although they are usually to be found under that heading in catalogues and reference books) because they have no woody stems; nor are they herbaceous, since their long, straight, sword-like leaves are not lost in winter.

To refer to a plant as perennial is merely to say that it lives for several seasons and does not die after flowering but lives on to flower again. In gardening we have come to apply this term 'perennial' only to plants that cannot be described as trees, shrubs, or bulbs; further, we have eliminated all but herbaceous plants from this category, so that 'perennial' presupposes 'herbaceous perennial', and have left out all anomalies. The answer is to re-establish the definition of perennial to include evergreen, non-woody plants. This is more accurate, too, as herbaceousness is a matter of degree. Many so-called herbaceous plants fail to die down in winter in places where frosts are infrequent (herbaceous penstemons, for instance) and they would be much better placed in the useful and clear-cut category of non-woody perennials.

Phormium tenax has huge leaves. They can be from 1.8 to 2.75m/6 to 9ft long and 12cm/5in wide, and are of a beautiful matt grey-green, with a narrow, orange-red line down each margin and on the midrib. They stand proudly erect in great, uncompromising clumps, flinging up 4.5m/15ft panicles of deep red, almost black-purple flowers. This is a magnificent accent plant that, if sheltered from cold winds, can prove very hardy. Its reputation for tenderness owes more to its demanding a dramatic site, and hence to its being habitually planted in exposed places, than to any innate sensitivity. It does not mind what soil it finds itself growing in, although the richer and moister its conditions, the larger it will grow.

Forms of *P. cookianum* are proportioned neatly enough for the small garden, and are part of the lower-level foliage in larger ones. Their leaves are from 60cm to 1.2m/24in to 4ft long but lack the rigidity and thespian élan of the larger species. They tend to droop from a break point, rather like a paper tube that has been made too long and cannot be held out straight. Although the species is the mountain flax, it is not as hardy as its larger relative when it comes to survival in cold gardens. There are many new and exciting forms with variegations in shades of red and yellow, but they should all be treated with caution.

The transition from dry to moist that began with yuccas and tiger grass and led on to *Phormium tenax* can be completed without losing sight of linear leaves and monocotyledons. The phormium's toleration of a wide variety of soils allows it to associate as happily with bamboos as with yuccas and other plants that like dry places. Bamboos are grasses that enjoy moist places, but they, too, are extremely tolerant, sometimes even of shallow, dry, calcareous soils. Bamboos are the least understood of all the groups of ornamental plants that we grow. This lack of understanding applies as much to their cultivation as to their rather odd lifestyles. Possibly only pandas really appreciate bamboos; gardeners do not – if they did, they would grow far more of these superb plants. Unfortunately, bamboos are thought of as plants that will not tolerate cold, and their tropical antecedents, real in the cases of many species but mythical in those of a great many more, lead them to be shunned by many gardeners in cool-temperate climates.

The lushness and admittedly tropical appearance of the canes and foliage of the hardy species lend an exotic note that is beyond the capabilities of any other plants. That they are hardy is beyond question; it is their intolerance of windy positions that has raised question marks against them. Bamboos cannot be used as primary windbreaks, although countless attempts have been made to use them for the purpose. As secondary shelter, though, they are superb, blocking almost entirely the winds that have already had their strengths considerably reduced by primary windbreaks. Within the garden – that is to say behind the first, main rank of wind-sheltering plants – the quality of bamboos is such that still, calm areas can be created which remain tranquil even when winds of considerable force are blowing outside. Their rustle and sway as they absorb the winds' energies do not detract from this, but rather enhance it.

Arundinaria japonica is perhaps the most widely cultivated of all bamboos where winters are cold. It is tall enough – up to 6m/18ft, but usually 4.5m/15ft – and is extremely hardy. The only trouble is that, after many decades of only the most spasmodic flowering, in which just the odd cane would join, recent years have seen the unusual phenomenon of a bamboo species flowering for three or more years running, and all year round at that. *A. japonica* looks terrible when it has flowered, with just the odd green leaf here and there amidst a mass of dead grey stuff, but it will regenerate if it is cut right down and given some manure and the blessing of a little patience on the part of its owner.

Many nonsenses are talked about in connection with the flowering of bamboos, the chief of which is that they die after flowering. Another is that every plant of a species, no matter where it is on earth, flowers in the same year. If this were true there would, of course, be no point at all in bamboos being perennials: it would be simpler and more efficient biologically for them to be annuals and to produce seed, apparently so vital to their survival, every year. That they *appear* to die after flowering is true; it is also true that gardeners are all too prone to condemn plant patients to death when a period of intensive care would restore them to full health.

Unfortunately, the mass flowering of *A. japonica* means that it will be a while before it can safely be recommended again, but there are other hardy species that are of even greater worth. A reliance on any one is to ask for a yawning gap for a few years; to diversify is to play safe. The straighter-growing bamboos are ideal middle-layer plants in that they can provide interior walls in the garden which hide one feature from another and act as partitions between scenes of totally different character. They are also the best backgrounds for the display of flowers, since, unlike those bamboos whose canes are more flexible, they do not arch over and keep rain and sun off the flowering plants.

Bamboos are not in the least snobbish or even élitist, and look equally appropriate showing off annuals like *Nicotiana*, perennials like *Cimicifuga*

Arundinaria viridistriata *is beautiful in its canes as well as its leaves. Long, erect, purplish stems bear foliage that is variegated with ochre yellow on a dark green background. A very hardy bamboo, but not at all invasive, it can safely be grown either in the open ground or in a tub.*

racemosa or shrubs like rhododendrons. If it were only realised how perfectly *Phyllostachys viridi-glaucescens* brings out the blue in the foliage of *Abies koreana* and emphasises the purple of its cones, if only the blousy blooms of highly-bred tree peonies could be seen in perfect juxtaposition with it, it would come into its own as one of the most desirable of garden plants. It is a tall species – up to 6m/18ft – and forms well-behaved thickets which are remarkably non-invasive. When it flowers, which it does with regularity but at decent intervals, it just gets a bit gappy for a few seasons but does not become ugly at all.

Arundinaria nitida is a plant that can be made suitable for gardens of any size simply by adjusting the number of specimens planted. Its propensity for running is minimal, and it will occupy much the same space for many years. Its slim, purplish canes bow elegantly under the weight of the narrow, grassy foliage, eventually almost touching the ground. It really does want to be a specimen and demands individual treatment. As a lawn plant, a clump will provide a place for children to hide and make adults wish that they still could. The more frequently found *A. murielae* is somewhat similar, with yellowish stems.

Before introducing a bamboo to the garden it is as well to take advice from a trustworthy plantsman or from a good book which deals with the genus, as there are thugs among them to whom a spot of pillage is as routine as it was to any pirate. Take for example *Sasa palmata*, which has broad leaves and bright green canes and would seem at first sight to be an ideal 'foliage' plant. Woe betide followers of the foliage-only school who seize on it for their gardens; it will in its turn seize the garden, taking over with the venomous determination of a cross between Brobdingnagian couch grass and a triffid.

It is slightly odd that the monocotyledons provide us with such rich foliage while most plants with the same linear leaves appear singularly unimpressive. There are few trees or shrubs – the rather tender *Crinodendron hookerianum* is an exception – which have linear foliage that could be called an asset. The genus *Salix*, which comprises the willows, has linear leaves among its constant characteristics, but tends to go in for elliptic leaves when it wants to impress. *Salix fargesii* is one of the exceptional ones and has quite broad, glossy green leaves with deeply impressed veins. Its brightly coloured winter buds make it valuable all year round and it is, at only 3m/10ft tall or so, an impressive subject for small gardens.

Willows should be grown for their barks and stems, rather than for their leaves. Their catkins can be extremely attractive, too, and are often borne before the leaves. Qualities of stems are, strictly speaking, nothing to do with foliage. We should be aware, however, that it is impossible to draw lines of absolute demarcation in nature, and it is a legitimate aspect of the study of foliage to examine the effects of its absence and ways of lessening or heightening these effects. Willows have some of the most deliciously coloured stems.

The tall bamboo Phyllostachys viridi-glaucescens *has bright leaves, shining green above and bluish below; the canes mature from green to dull yellow. In larger gardens it can be used to make curtains of foliage for creating surprises, or marking subdivisions.*

It is almost as if Nature were trying to compensate for providing them with undistinguished leaves which only seem to be effective when they are weeping.

The garden in the Cold can be transformed by the presence of a willow such as *S. daphnoides*, whose shoots are deep purple under a white bloom. It is not often seen in garden centres, but it roots easily from long hardwood cuttings which you might well obtain from the same source as the basketmakers do. They call it 'French Purple', and weave it in to create blocks or strands of contrasting colour. *Salix* 'Decipiens' is a small tree with reddish-orange shoots. In other species this colour varies from dark red to light yellow. Blue shoots occur in species such as *S. irrorata*, and occasionally a willow with bright green winter branches can be found. They are all superb seen in company with white-stemmed birches and the yellow- and red-stemmed European dogwoods.

The finest willow of all for foliage is *S. magnifica*, whose large leaves are for all the world like those of a magnolia. Its catkins disabuse you of the notion that it is a magnolia, however, and are among the longest and most intriguing to be found. The leaves are anything but linear and serve as another example of how it is no good looking for that shape among dicotyledons if you expect anything special at all.

Conifers with linear foliage – and there are many of them – rely on the mass effect of their leaves. Each individual leaf is a non-event, whether it is the long, grey needle of the maritime pine or the short, blunt chisel that grows on the branchlet of a species of *Abies*. The overall effect is that of foliage as opposed to leaves.

It is only at the middle level and below that we can begin to see conifer foliage as anything other than undifferentiated masses. In the upper layer the foliage is just too high up for our eyes to distinguish anything very much other than that the pines look as though they are made of masses of brushes. Even when conifer foliage presents itself to us at eye level, we still tend to take little notice of it as leaves. It is still the shapes that intrigue us, although we may find interest in the way branches behave rather than the tree as a whole. We grow conifers for their shapes and the colours of their foliage. Those who are keen on plants may well look closely at a leaf of an *Abies* species and appreciate its deep, almost olive-green upper surface and whitely silver lower one, but they grow it for the effect such leaves have in their many thousands. Each little chisel is only capable of playing crowd scenes.

Berberis darwinii, *with its small simple leaves, is a structureless shrub that somehow achieves poise and a certain elegance.*

Small leaves

Large-leaved plants provide us with explanations for their effects – whether they are pinnate or entire, for instance. One can quite readily say that the effect of certain large-leaved plants is heavy and jungly, of others majestic or dignified. It is not so with plants whose small leaves are clustered into masses. Neither is it possible to decide that they have characteristic shapes that have effects, unless they are conifers or have been clipped. *Berberis darwinii* has no definite shape; it is not rounded, nor hummock-making, nor anything very much, yet it is an extremely effective shrub at all times of the year and never more so than when in gorgeous orange flower. Clipped for a hedge it takes on whatever shape is imposed upon it.

The shrubby potentillas have small, densely set leaves and flowers that are well known for their brightness and size. Few people, however, would claim for them any distinction of foliage or out-of-flower charm; they are also devoid of definable shape. Try, however, to describe in factual terms what it is that makes the berberis foliage so attractive and that of the potentillas so dull and you will fail to convince.

Plants with small leaves may be regarded primarily as space-fillers – meant not in the pejorative sense reserved for *Ajuga* and *Vinca*, which are bought by the unimaginative to fill countless thousands of gaps, but in a positive and constructive one. Planted between and behind plants with prominent characteristics such as white bark, as well as those with large leaves, they lend substance and solidity to the garden, help to divide it up and create surprises, act as a backcloth to flowers and, if well chosen, add a note of discreet grace and subtlety to the general flamboyant floral display.

It should not be forgotten, however, that there are small-leaved plants of the middle layer whose individual leaves are worth close inspection. This is rarely because of some beauty in the miniature, but is more likely because of some curiosity value, although individual tastes will enter into things, as always. The hedgehog holly, *Ilex aquifolium* 'Ferox', is definitely one of the more curious. Every tiny leaf has spines all over its upper surface as well as along its margins and is rather like a miniature hedgehog in green porcelain. *I.a.* 'Ferox Argentea' has cream margins and spines; *I.a.* 'Ferox Aurea' has even smaller leaves strongly marked with gold, and is so slow-growing that it hardly reaches above knee-height even after many years. Ignoring these fascinating if rather monstrous leaves is to miss one of gardening's more interesting curiosities, although there is more purpose to their presence than mere museum value: they make one of the densest and most anti-social hedges imaginable.

Beauty in individual small leaves is exemplified by another holly, *Ilex pernyi*. This is a stiff shrub, 3m/10ft or more in height, which is typically holly-like in habit, even though its leaves are fascinatingly different from those of other hollies. They are rather like small ornamental arrowheads, with formal, almost heraldic shapes such as might have been devised for a medieval king. Each leaf is

ABOVE *Hedges are at their most plastic as a sculptural medium when consisting of dense masses of small, uncomplicated leaves.*

LEFT *The evergreen leaves of* Itea ilicifolia *are only moderately holly-like, as many are unspined, while a few are smooth-edged. In late summer this attractive shrub is laden with long, tassel-like catkins.*

only about 2.5cm/1in long, but will stay in the memory for a much longer period of time than many larger ones.

Perhaps the greatest curiosity in the world of foliage is its almost total absence. Some plants have no leaves at all, or just a few rudimentary ones. The leaves of other plants have become smaller and smaller until they have almost vanished, having been converted at some stage in their evolution into spines, or had their functions usurped by stems. The knowledgeable might at this stage point out that yet other plants have structures – namely phyllodes – that are like leaves and have their function. Fair enough. In practice the origin of a leaf-like structure makes little difference; if it looks like a leaf it will behave like a leaf.

Spines and naked green stems are not leaf-like at all but are, paradoxically, part of the garden foliage. A dense thicket of spines has the same visual effect as a crowded mass of tiny leaves – physically, however, the effect is quite different, and it is not a good idea to place a plant like *Colletia armata* near a path, or *C. cruciata*, armed with wickedly barbed knives, where children might stumble across it. Nevertheless, both of these plants are beautiful. The sharp, branched bodkins of *C.armata* are redolent of hot, dry places and, sure enough, it enjoys growing on a sunny, well-drained bank, where it can associate with cistuses or make the most vivid and intriguing contrast with *Cytisus battandieri*. Both species are valuable for their very late flowers, which are usually white – pink in *C. armata* 'Rosea'. These are small but where summers are warm they are borne in great numbers all along the branches. Winters have to be severe to harm them, so it is hard to see what it is other than their unsociable spines that makes them so uncommon in gardens.

Brooms lack leaves almost completely, which may make them rather more like flower-carriers than real thorough-going plants, but they are useful in helping to create a Mediterranean atmosphere, particularly when associated with other leafless plants and with those more leafy ones that also speak of hot, dry hillsides and maquis-type vegetation.

TOP *The smooth rounded leaves of* Cotinus coggygria *are instantly recognisable.*

ABOVE *The humble* Cotoneaster horizontalis *demonstrates that beauty is not the sole prerogative of the spectacular or rare. The ranks of small leaves in their herringbone patterns are exquisitely picked out by frost.*

Large leaves

Plants with large leaves naturally conjure up visions of hot places. The Japanese loquat, *Eriobotrya japonica*, has 30cm/12in long leaves like corrugated leather that will be familiar to those who have spent time in the Mediterranean regions of the world, where this plant is grown for its delicious fruits. It flowers only where summers are hot, and the blooms are borne in winter, so the sole reason for growing it in less balmy climates is for its leaves. These are more like those of a rhododendron than anything else. My plants grow among camellias and rhododendrons in a grassy dell and look perfectly at home.

Rhododendron itself is a genus of the greatest variety, among whose members are tiny, dwarf shrubs no more than 2.5 to 5cm/1 to 2in high and giants whose dimensions vie with those of large trees. Leaf size, too, varies enormously. At the top of the range are the so-called large-leaved rhododendrons – not a botanical grouping but merely a gardening category – which are some of the most telling plants for foliage that can be grown.

R. sinogrande is the doyen of them all. A young plant will often have leaves nearly 90cm/36in long and 30cm/12in wide. They are something like those of the rubber plant, *Ficus elastica*, but are even larger; sometimes as much as twice as large. A young plant of 1.8m/6ft or so in height is a major feature in a small garden and a significant one even in a larger space. A mature tree is a truly splendid sight, especially in the spring, when its huge trusses of cream-white flowers transform it into an enormous chandelier. The undersides of the leaves are covered with a silvery indumentum of tightly adpressed hairs. This does not appear hairy at all, but as if the lower surface of the leaf were plated in silver. The light-reflecting quality of hollow hairs is such that their arrangement gives an impression of whiteness. This phenomenon is seen in the leaves of many other kinds of plants.

Rhododendron fans are often called 'leaf turners' because of their habit of looking at the leaf undersides. Many rhododendrons grow tall enough for their undersides to be displayed up above eye level. Others, like *R. fulvum*, make denser shrubs with leaves set at all sorts of different angles so that at once you see the olive-green upper surfaces of some and the chocolate-tawny underparts of others.

ABOVE Rhododendron macabeanum *is perhaps the hardiest and most reliable of all the large-leaved rhododendrons. The undersides of newly emergent foliage are a pure silvery white.*

Rhododendron falconeri has leaves that are almost as large as those on older plants of *R. sinogrande*, but are matt instead of glossy on top and of a lighter green with a hint of yellow in it that produces an almost khaki hue. The undersides are felted, not silky, with brown-tan indumentum. Its flower-trusses are enormous, the flowers a light, creamy yellow with the maroon basal blotches so often characteristic of the large-leaved rhododendrons. *R. eximium* is similar, but its leaves are darker underneath and not quite as large, although they are usually over 30cm/12in long, which is large by any standards. *R. arizelum* maintains the theme of brown undersides, but is just about the smallest-leaved of the group.

Woolly, white indumentum is found on the reverses of the leaves of *R. macabeanum*. This is the member of the large-leaved group that is seen most often in cultivation, partly because it is capable of withstanding drier, less humid conditions than the others. All these rhododendrons are much hardier than is generally supposed, and this one is the most tolerant of a wide range of conditions. Although they will endure cold, none of them will tolerate cold winds, so they should always be grown in sheltered conditions.

OPPOSITE *The young leaves of* Pieris 'Forest Flame' *are bright flame red. As they age, they turn gradually to a shrimp pink and then to creamy white before they become suffused with the adult green.*

It ought to be seen as axiomatic that any plant with large evergreen leaves will need shelter from wind, but it is not. Few gardeners have had it pointed out to them that it is not cold *per se* that kills plants – it is drying out. Cold winds with frozen soil are anathema to evergreens. If they are mulched to keep their roots moist and unfrozen and sheltered to protect their leaves from desiccation, many plants will be found to be 'hardy' that were previously written off as tender. Large-leaved rhododendrons flower early in the year while there may still be a threat of frost, so it is just as well if they are grown in the first instance for their leaves, and their flowers regarded only as a bonus to be enjoyed in favourable years. The primrose-yellow bells of *R. macabeanum*, many to a very large truss, are worth waiting for. Meanwhile you can turn over the new leaves and be dazzled by the snowy whiteness that lies beneath, or be intrigued by the older ones, which have the colour and texture of the backs of shorn sheep.

Rhododendron arboreum is a tree-like species whose flowers will survive only in mild areas, but which could with complete justification be grown for its foliage alone. Depending upon what part of its range it comes from, its leaf-reverses will vary from a thin felt of wonderfully rich russet-brown to a thin skim of pure, shiny silver, and the deep impression of the veins makes them stand out sharply, adding a herringbone pattern to the colours. When the plants get to be taller than you are, they are one of the most beautiful sights in the garden. If your climate is mild enough to support *R. arboreum* flowers, you can also grow some of its hybrids to flowering. One word of warning applies: do not on any account grow the red forms of the species near any of its several red, early-flowering hybrids. The scarlet purity of *R. arboreum* itself will set up the most unholy clash with the blue in the red of almost all the hybrids. This does not apply to the Hardy Hybrids, which flower almost two months later.

Becoming a rhododendron leaf-turner is not a bad idea, as it is good training for the rest of your life as a foliage-lover. You will find yourself unable to pass a tasty-looking leaf without looking to see what lies underneath. Sometimes you will find nothing but aphids, but often you will be

Above Photinia *'Red Robin' provides a startling contrast to* Philadelphus coronarius *'Aureus'.*

Right With its magnificent flowers and fresh but tropical-looking green leaves, the hardy evergreen Magnolia grandiflora *adds a touch of the exotic to a temperate garden.*

rewarded and will come to value plants such as the olearias and even the smaller *Rhododendron* species such as *R. yakushimanum*. The large-leaved rhododendrons are, too, a school for those who have not yet learned to appreciate the beauty of young, unfurling foliage. We tend to rave about autumn colour, but when did you last hear someone extolling the virtues of the clean, white green of newly-born rhododendron leaves? So often leaves which are destined to become quite ordinary for the rest of their lives have a few early days of glory, and fleeting as such phenomena may be, they are an important part of the foliage scene. The effect of the bright red young leaves of *Pieris* 'Forest Flame', for example, is one of the most spectacular that garden foliage can provide. And the new growths of *Photinia* 'Red Robin' are equally brilliant.

Wherever one goes, magnolias are enormously popular. It is easy to be ecstatic about their flowers, whether they are the small, strap-petalled ones of *M. stellata* or the huge water-lily blooms of *M. campbellii* or its variety *M.c.* var. *mollicomata. M. delavayi* produces its wide, waxen, creamy-yellow flowers off and on for weeks in summer, while good flowering forms of *M. grandiflora* astonish us with the opulence of their great blossoms in early autumn. That such wonderful flower-bearers should also be among the very best for large, simple leaves not too far above eye level is one of the plant kingdom's most generous gifts.

M. grandiflora is a native of southeastern American forests, whose floors may be found to be liberally scattered with its seedlings, and is one of the best of all garden shrubs and trees. In cultivation it tends to be shrubby because it is so susceptible to the weight of snow that it does not have a chance to attain tree height. For this reason its charms grace the middle layer and are near to our eyes where they may be best appreciated. Its flowers are deliciously fragrant, creamy in colour, and can be up to 20cm/8in across. The leathery leaves, which, like those of *Rhododendron falconeri* are glossy green with that hint of yellow that suggests khaki, are an important addition to the evergreen element of foliage wherever it can be grown, which is almost anywhere provided that the old enemy, cold wind, is kept out. The

Parrotia persica *is especially valued for its brilliant autumn colour, in tones of gold and red. Though its leaves are not especially large, they are big enough for their individual shapes to stand out from the mass.*

well-trained leaf-turner will soon spot the rusty-brown indumentum beneath the leaves, even though it may not last the full season.

As a rule (and it is by no means hard and fast) the more and longer-lasting the indumentum, the less likely is the plant to flower before it is rather old. The best counsel is to grow a form that has long-lasting, well-coloured undersides to the leaves and wait the twenty years or so for the first flowers. If everyone pursues only the flowers, these fine forms will be lost.

M. grandiflora will tolerate and even thrive on the most lime-charged soils, provided there is plenty of vegetable matter present. On the other hand, the species which carries the largest leaves of any deciduous tree or shrub that can be grown in cool-temperate or maritime continental climates needs complete freedom from lime. This is *M. macrophylla*, whose thin leaves are arranged in parasol-like whorls and are about 60cm/24in long. It is one of a group of three species which are summer-flowering, large-leaved, and not grown as widely as they might be. None of them makes a large tree, and all are of great beauty and capable of withstanding severe winters as long as their roots are well mulched in autumn to protect them from the damage penetrating frosts can wreak.

M. hypoleuca and *M. officinalis*, the other two in this group, are almost identical to *M. macrophylla* in leaf, but *M. officinalis* var. *biloba* has leaves like no others. They are large, obovate and conspicuously notched at their ends to give a two-lobed effect. Where the climate is severe, the large-leaved magnolia of choice is the umbrella tree, *M. tripetala*. Leaves of well over 30cm/12in long are arranged in whorls that come close to appearing like huge digitately-compound leaves, and the flowers – again borne in summer – have a heady scent.

Variegated Foliage

Variegated foliage needs to be quite close to our eyes for us to be able to appreciate the fact that it is variegated at all. Further away, it looks merely light in colour and tends to merge with the other light green and yellow tones. It is, therefore, in the middle layer that we first notice variegation. Tall trees with parti-coloured leaves are uncommon in any case, but become ineffective when they reach maturity and can only be examined through binoculars.

Variegated plants are the food and drink of the foliage-only school and of those who seek out what they are pleased to call 'foliage plants'. This is not a bad thing; what is bad is the obsessive tendencies that go with it. Gardens with an over-concentration of striped, speckled, zoned and bedashed leaves are unnerving, restless-feeling places lacking both harmony and balance. Yet variegated foliage continues to be thoroughly overdone and some pretty nasty-looking plants achieve large sales and appear in garden after garden. Again it comes down to individual taste. While many people delight in *Berberis* 'Rose Glow' – and who shall deny them – I find it to be one of the two most repulsive plants that I know. Its leaves are smeared with pink and maroon in a way that reminds me of the jelly and ice-cream that adhere to plates after a five-year-old's birthday party. Yet somehow I sense that I must be wrong, as I see it in almost every shrub border I visit.

The other of my two least favourites is *Prunus laurocerasus* 'Marble White'. This evergreen

shrub, of stunted and dense habit, is beloved by flower arrangers but thoroughly hated by me. Its sickly, twisted, narrow leaves are streaked and spotted with white on a light green background and the bush has no shape other than that of an amorphous blob – fitting it in with other plants is to attempt the impossible. Wherever it is put it remains an excrescence.

I cannot begin to suggest a use in the garden for plants that I find ugly, but can only advise that you look for yourself and use them if you like. What I would ask, though, is that variegation be restrained. It will be much more effective and the plants will look more natural if they are placed sparingly. This is not simply a matter of taste; it has to do with harmonious composition.

One of the best characteristics of variegated plants is that they can be used to introduce points of light into the foliage scene. The play of colour among the many shades of green, the purples, silvers and golds, is one of the gradation from one tone to another, sometimes punctuated by the out-of-phase positioning of a bright note among more sombre passages. Variegation can be used to introduce further accents of light, and also to say something fresh about the background tones. The even, darkish greens that so often occur in places in the garden that are both shady and rather dry can be boring. Dry shade is difficult at the best of times; to attempt to create a drama out of it might appear difficult but can be done using one of the toughest and most commonly-grown shrubs of all. This is *Elaeagnus pungens* 'Maculata', a bright customer which has been the subject of heavy doses of horticultural snobbery.

Woe betide the plant that becomes universally popular! Those who seek to be the arbiters of taste will drop it like a hot coal once they see it in too many gardens, and they will decry their erstwhile darling at every opportunity: 'You don't grow *that* rubbishy old thing!' Well, I do, because it is a vigorous, hardy shrub that tolerates just about any soil and position, and its broadly oval leaves outline in dark green the brilliant gold shields displayed at their centres. What is more, the brightness this plant creates in a shady spot is accentuated when sunlight reaches it. The gold shines out sensationally then, and what was a relatively dull part of the garden is allowed to play its own vital part in the foliage display.

This shrub will eventually take up rather a lot of room (although it can be pruned back), but small gardens can be equally well decorated by the variety *E.p.* 'Dicksonii'. This is slower-growing and more upright than its sprawling relation, but is equally at home in adverse conditions. The variegation consists of a broad band of gold round the edge of each leaf, rather than a zone in the middle. Either plant, because it has a dark green part to the leaf, picks up the background colour of a dry, shady planting, making a statement about that colour and showing us that dark green looks pretty good when there is some powerful gold about. Similarly, *Phormium tenax* 'Variegatum' will offset grey-green plants, but it does not do to be too clever, for good enough effects will be obtained by using variegated plants as highlights in their own right without forcing their hands in other directions.

The variegated phormiums are not as hardy as the type and will often be cut to ground level by severe winters. Quite a few gardeners, knowing these shrubs are evergreen, assume that they have been killed outright, forgetting the old rule that no plant should be written off as dead until midsummer is past. These phormiums will usually send up some tentative, scouting shoots to see if it is safe above and will then get on with refurbishing themselves. They should be protected the next winter, as they will not have ripened enough to survive a second dose of deadly cold. They are slower-growing than the type as well, and therefore illustrate the general rule that variegated plants are slower in growth than their green equivalents. The reason for this is fairly simple. Variegation implies a reduction of the normal amount of chlorophyll in the leaves and thus a lessening of the process of photosynthesis by which plants use light to turn carbon dioxide and water into sugar and starch. Placing a plant such as *Weigela florida* 'Variegata' among other weigelas for contrast would seem at first to be an excellent idea, but it does not work because of the slow growth rate of the variegated plant *vis à vis* its green relatives. The best use for it is among plants such as hydrangeas whose stature is similar (although the larger lacecaps should be avoided) and whose broad, plain leaves contrast strongly with its own narrow, creamily variegated ones. Furthermore, the pink flowers of the weigela, no smaller than those of the green forms, will have bloomed while the hydrangeas are still waiting to do so.

ABOVE A gardener who appreciates foliage properly will take every opportunity to bring leaves and flowers together. Here, Clematis macropetala *decorates and embellishes* Elaeagnus pungens *'Maculata'.*

The fact that green plant material grows faster than the variegated kind makes reversion that much more dangerous. Reversion is a process whereby a plant, normally variegated, puts out branches that are green. These branches grow very quickly and appear to have a coarse mien, and can often take over completely, reducing the variegated branches to nothing or to a mere rump. It is important that anything with variegated foliage should be watched and any reverting material pruned away as soon as possible. Such is the degree of reversion in some plants that they have to be regarded in the end as not worth growing. Among these are two variegated snowberries, *Symphoricarpos orbiculatus* 'Variegatus' and another in the same species that appears in no reference work and has silver variegation instead of gold. They both revert like crazy, and it is a shame, as their little, spoon-shaped leaves have the gold or silver around the edges of their otherwise grey-green leaves. When the green shoots get going

OPPOSITE Some of the best variegated shrubs are also very fine when in flower. Weigela florida *'Variegata' has pretty, light pink flowers in late spring. The foliage is stronger, bolder and more markedly variegated if the plant is pruned quite hard, but the pruning should be done just after flowering, so that the following year's flowers will not be lost.*

ABOVE Actinidia kolomikta *is grown solely for the spectacular variegation of its foliage: the terminal half of each leaf is flushed pink over creamy white.*

OPPOSITE A delightfully interrelated planting: Hedera helix *'Gold Heart' and* H.h. *'Marginata' have one another's variegation in reverse, and a subtle distinction of colour.* Euonymus *'Emerald and Gold' is balanced by the gentler variegation of the hosta. The yucca's leaves echo the ivies' colours and draw sharpness from their association with the soft fronds of the fern.*

they are rampant and even if they are removed the plants seem unable to cope with having to try again.

Reversion becomes a thoroughgoing nuisance when it occurs in trees. Among the worst offenders are forms of box elder such as *Acer negundo* 'Variegatum'. I have not been growing 'Flamingo' long enough to know whether it will be as bad as its slightly plainer relative, but I shall keep an eye on it, as there is bad blood there which comes out in the form of reverted shoots at the precise height which prevents their being tackled from my ladder. Faults in plants are something that the gardener can put up with; sheer vindictiveness is quite another thing.

Of all the variegated trees, *Acer platanoides* 'Drummondii' appeals to me most. It is, of course, slow-growing, and fits perfectly into the middle layer of the larger garden. In the small garden it makes a fine major specimen, and is worth a place of honour anywhere, especially as it likes sun. Some friends who have a zoological garden have some beautiful, domed specimens out in the open, where the silvery leaves, each outlined with a white band, do wonders for the pinks of the flamingos. This, too, will suddenly deliver itself of a branch whose pure green shows its Norway maple origins – such things must be removed with haste before a nasty gap is made in the tree's crown.

The hydrangeas, cited as foils for the variegated weigela, have among their number a plant of great beauty whose variegated foliage never seems to revert at all. It is a bit of a mystery, too, and is such a good plant that this mystery deserves some tentative unravelling. Many nursery lists and reference books will mention a lacecap hydrangea with light pink flowers and variegated leaves as *H.* 'Tricolor'. Thereafter they part company, some saying the three colours of the leaves are grey, green and white, while others declare them to be grey, green and gold. In fact, the colours are grey, green, white *and* gold, and there are four of them and not three. The correct name of the plant is 'Quadricolor' and there is, I believe, no such cultivar as 'Tricolor'. If it is grown badly, or is running out of nutrients, the colours will be grey, green and white, and it will thus appear three-coloured. Only the gold disappears, however; the plant never shows itself clothed in grey, green and gold without some white being present.

This superb hydrangea is attractive for a large part of the year and in mild winters will remain evergreen for ten months or so. What is more, its heads of delicate pink flowers remain in good condition right into the winter. Where possible its ideal companions are the smaller eucryphias, whose dark green, exquisitely-shaped, densely-packed leaves balance beautifully the much larger, gracefully variegated ones of the hydrangea.

There is a similarity between the hydrangea's leaves and those of the variegated forms of the Asian dogwoods that precludes their being grown together. The dogwoods will grow in almost any conditions, from damp to dry, but it is as well to let them have plenty of sun. They are common enough plants, especially the Siberian *Cornus alba*, whose variegated forms are the subject of much confusion as to name. This tends to happen with plants given pseudo-Latin cultivar names; one, the most commonly grown, has been in its

ABOVE *With its interesting tabulated structure,* Cornus controversa *'Variegata' is attractive even after its beautifully silver-variegated leaves have fallen. In leaf it is superb.*

OPPOSITE Hedera helix *'Buttercup' is the best of the gold-variegated ivies. Its young leaves show no green, but become greener as they age.*

time *C.a. sibirica*, 'Sibirica Variegata', *argenteo-marginata* and, most recently and acceptably, 'Elegantissima'.

Before talking about this robust and easy plant, let us clear the decks of all other names that may appear in catalogues and lead you to the wrong plant. *C.a.* 'Gouchaltii' is valid, but is a poor plant with a dim attempt at being prettily variegated. 'Tricolor' and 'Froebellii' probably do not exist, and 'Sibirica' is a different form which is neither variegated nor as tough. For our purposes we can reduce the desirable plants to two – *C.a.* 'Elegantissima' and *C.a.* 'Spaethii'. Both have red stems that are of the utmost value in the Cold, making thickets of whippy sticks that look wonderful on chilly days, especially when the sun shines on them. You would be torn between placing them either for these wintry benefits or so that their variegated leaves give of their best. 'Elegantissima' has grey-green leaves with creamy margins, while 'Spaethii' is brightly variegated with gold. Perhaps 'Elegantissima' is best with some shade at midday, as it can become scorched. 'Spaethii' does not suffer from this and can be allowed all the sun it can take. Either is ideal by a pond, where the stems and the foliage can be reflected in the water's surface.

The tendency to become scorched is another common weakness of variegated plants. This is not to say that they are unhealthy, they are just more genetically inclined to be affected by extremes. It would be unwise to over-emphasise genetics in connection with variegated plants. Very few come true from seed, and it is as well always to propagate from cutting or division. Here again, though, a note of caution must be sounded. Some variegations are caused by disease. The condition is known as infectious chlorosis and it is usually transmitted from one plant to another, although in an entirely haphazard way. Viruses and other agents cause the condition, often using the agency of sap-sucking insects, but sometimes it is gardeners themselves who unwittingly allow their knives to be the agents of infection. Camellias suffer from a bright yellow, irregular variegation that is caused by a virus. This is readily spread, and lack of hygiene when taking cuttings can soon disfigure large numbers of plants. It is as well never to attempt to propagate a variegated shoot from a camellia, no matter how fetching it may seem. The same applies to abutilons, *Fraxinus, Sorbus* and several other genera.

The collector of variegations may well have an inadvertently deleterious effect on neighbouring gardens. No matter how keen you are on a new plant, it is as well to make sure that you are happy with its antecedents. Another pitfall is the vast number of cultivars that are harmless and attractive enough but which are not really sufficiently distinct and should never have been distributed in the first place. The result is that garden planners find themselves faced with a plethora of names and not much guidance as to which plants will suit the purpose.

The hollies provide a prize example of this. Of *Ilex aquifolium* alone I am able to find just over thirty names of cultivars with variegation, many of which are synonyms. This is crazy, especially when horrors such as 'Aurea Mediopicta Latifolia' are perpetrated. Luckily, this one is better known as 'Golden Milkboy', a fine, large-leaved plant with the more unusual type of variegation in hollies – a splash of gold in the centre of each leaf. 'Golden Queen' demonstrates the more commonly-found pattern of a golden band around the leaf – in this case accompanied by shading of the green in the centre. Life is never simple, however, and

this queen is a male and will never bear berries. 'Silver Queen' is variegated with white, and is worth growing in spite of the fact that it is also, maddeningly, a male. To obtain a berried holly with variegation, try *Ilex* × *altaclarensis* 'Golden King'. Its user-friendly, almost spineless leaves have broad golden margins around them. The catch is that this king is a female! When the berries of a holly are so desirable, it is difficult to understand what possesses people to set nomenclatural traps such as these.

Perhaps the sternest warning that one can give in connection with variegated plants is that it is very easy to become heartily sick of them. They require more careful placing in the garden than almost anything else, precisely because they are so different and attract so much attention. Happily and harmoniously placed, patterned leaves are an asset to the foliage picture, and even essential to it. One job that they do well is to form links with and pointers to other colours throughout the garden. The light gold at the leaf centre of the ivy *Hedera helix* 'Gold Heart' will relate well to a *Philadelphus coronarius* 'Aureus' a little way off. The very small leaves of *Azara microphȳlla* 'Variegata' (if you can find it) can be made to connect with the very large ones of the similarly yellow-variegated, pinnate ones of *Aralia elata* 'Aureovariegata' (if you can afford it).

Growing *Fatsia japonica* 'Variegata' is fun for its own sake. The edges of the leaves and tips of their lobes are creamy white, and it is just as hardy as the plain form. Plant it not too far away from *Ilex aquifolium* 'Handsworth New Silver', whose dark green leaves are margined with the same creamy white, and you will have created a starting point for a whole series of relationships of leaf-shapes and colours that can quite easily develop into a comprehensive garden design. Harmony will best result when colour elements, including the variegated foliage, relate to their neighbours and to plants that are further away. Such relationships may not be visible from all angles; some viewpoints may obscure many of them. Nonetheless, their establishment will ensure a cohesion of design and give the garden an overall integrity that will be evident from any aspect.

Flowers, Fruits and Berries

Flowers play their parts in the establishment of harmonious plant relationships. Indeed, badly placed, or not thought about at the design stage, flowers can ruin the most elegant foliage concepts. To forget that the most colourful elements in a garden are the flowers is to risk the total eclipsing of your most cherished and subtle fancies.

In the middle layer, flowers compete strongly with foliage. After all, you expect to see flowers in a garden, and most of them will be at or below eye-level. Unless you revert to being a foliage-only gardener, you will want to have a myriad of blossoms around you. What you will try to do is minimise the incidence of negative effects upon the foliage arrangement that you have so carefully, and for such a long time, contrived. Take, for example, yellow foliage. Although it is called yellow, and often referred to as gold, it never stands up well to anything that is really and truly yellow. There is always a hint or overlay of brownish or greenish tones.

I have visited a garden where a hedge of *Lonicera nitida* 'Baggesen's Gold' looked nice and bright until summer. It is a shrub whose only use is as a fairly neat, dense, small-leaved hedge which will be golden if it gets plenty of light. Its great advantage is that it will grow absolutely anywhere and it is as hardy as a hobo. However, in this case, a group of shrubby, large-flowered hypericums – *H.* 'Hidcote' or 'Rowallane' – planted right in front of it made it look hopelessly inadequate. Their flowers were saucer-shaped and of the purest, sunniest yellow. The lonicera, hitherto glowing like burnished brass, was reduced to looking dirty, its gold degraded to a muddy khaki and what green there was in it showing up strongly. Blue flowers, or white ones, pink blooms or even red would have worked here, but yellow? Never!

A simple clash of flower colour can destroy good foliage relationships by taking the observer's attention away from them. This may sound elementary, but accidents do happen. The owner of a cosy, walled garden not far from the sea planted *Osmanthus heterophyllus* 'Variegatus' among a small group of camellias in order to make a year-round statement about the shininess and deep greenness of the camellia foliage. The osmanthus has holly-like foliage but differs from the hollies in that its leaves are more slender and lie opposite one another along the stems. Its matt, greyish-green leaves are prettily margined with white. The contrast with the camellias was perfect, and the fact that the plants were evergreen and of much the same stature made them complementary as well.

Camellias have a habit of flowering in the cuttings tray before they have rooted. They will usually flower in their first year or two as plants but will often refuse to flower until some years after being planted out. They seem to want to get

The flower spikes of Cotinus coggygria *demonstrate the aptness of the name 'smoke tree'. The foliage scene, if well planned, can support a dominant floral presence without losing its integrity.*

on with building themselves up first. Thus it was that this little group of plants reached considerable maturity before flowers played any part in the springtime display. When eventually the camellias in this garden started into full bloom, it became hard not to wish that they would soon give up and go away. Two of them were in harmony with one another – the brilliant, almost scarlet semi-double flowers of 'Alexander Hunter' went well with the soft sugar-pink of the similarly shaped blooms of 'Lady Clare' – it was the third that did the damage.

'Debbie', a universal favourite, has frilly, peony-form flowers that are pink with a hard blue tone in it. The effect on the other two was a total disaster. The clash shrieked so violently that all hope of the clever juxtaposition of foliage being noticed had to be postponed until flowering was over. Unfortunately, too, this was a small garden. There was nowhere to move 'Debbie', and so it stayed, to wreak its aesthetic havoc year after year.

It is of course true that, in comparison with foliage, flowers appear only fleetingly on the garden scene. We must nevertheless remember when designing with foliage that we ignore the influence of flowers at our peril. One violent clash is forgivable, but the gardener who creates one each season is going to have a problem, especially if the garden is small.

In the middle layer it is not only flowers that create outstanding colour; there are also fruits and berries. Here there is no real worry about disharmony, for foliage should be consciously used to show off fruits. Autumn colour and fruits go hand-in-hand and usually complement one another perfectly. Fruits last longer than deciduous foliage, though, and they can be left hanging nakedly, blackly outlined against the sky. Wherever possible they should be provided with an evergreen background.

I have a large plant of *Cotoneaster* 'Rothschildianus', 4.5m/15ft high, whose long, arching branches do not carry enough evergreen leaves to display adequately its large clusters of soft yellow berries. Most of the time the berries go unnoticed because I have not provided a background against which they can be seen. Such are circumstances in that part of the garden – a preponderance of deciduous trees and shrubs – that I am not going to be able to do much about it. It is not a moot point: the whole plant looks as if it is in the wrong place, and I shall have to try to move it, even if it means reducing its branch structure by more than half.

While the colours and structures of flowers are important to the success or failure of designing with foliage at the middle level of the garden, it is at ground level that they take over a leading role and can quite simply drown out any foliage. For this reason, the use of foliage at knee height and below is an art in itself; a difference in perception comes into play that is even more marked than that between the upper and middle layers.

The hardy sea buckthorn, Hippophae rhamnoides, *is a good addition to the middle layer, contributing silvery grey leaves in the Warm and brilliant orange-yellow berries in the Cold. The berries are unattractive to birds and last well into the winter.*

THE · LOWER · LAYER

Grasses, Perennials & Shrubs

The lower layer of foliage is not one in which we should abandon our search for colour and shape. Subtlety is as important in the creation of variety here as anywhere else, perhaps more so, for what is grown at ground level will determine to a large extent what kind of a garden one is looking at. The trees and shrubs of the upper and middle layers set atmosphere and character, but the lower layer demonstrates the hand of the gardener in a most direct way.

Two gardens, identical in every way in the composition of their upper two layers, will feel similar and be subject to the same play of light and air, while the proportions of open space to wooded areas will be the same. Radical differences in the way in which the garden floors are planted will not alter these, but they will greatly affect the style of the gardens.

Take, for instance, a garden in which there are some tall trees, graduating down to larger and then smaller shrubs, and that this arrangement is carried out on three sides of the 2000sqm/half-acre site. The fourth side is open to fields and faces the sun. There is a wealth of foliage interest among the shrubs and trees, with coloured patches illuminating the many greens and with leaves of all sizes and shapes used harmoniously. The open area enclosed by the trees and shrubs is grassy. The grass has been left alone so that now, in high summer, it is flowering and long. Amongst it appear some tall flowers – campanulas, foxgloves and loosestrife – and there is a sparse network of paths made by those who have strolled through and flattened the grass. Everywhere there is the hum of bees, the skitter of butterflies and the indefinable aroma of summer.

The lower layer can be as rich and varied as any other. Here links have been made with the middle layer in the background, using both large-leaved subjects and rhododendrons, while the lower-layer planting displays a theme of hostas.

The property is sold. A couple of years later, the same trees and shrubs grow in the same ways as before. Another lazy summer's day sees the open area formalised into a stretch of mown, bright green lawn, punctuated by island beds and almost surrounded by wavy borders. There is a mass of colour from herbaceous perennials and roses, among which are plants whose foliage stands out and helps to complement and display the myriad flowers. There are well-laid-out paths, edged with stones. There is a pond upon whose surface water-lilies glow on their rafts of round leaves and around the edges of which grows a mass of moisture-loving, large-leaved perennials.

In winter – in the depth of the Cold – this garden used to be carpeted in brownish grass, interestingly humped and hummocked and with last summer's paths showing as green tracks among the rougher herbiage. Now it is nothing like that. There is a stretch of lawn. There are beds where herbaceous perennials have gone to ground. The paths are neat and tidy and the pond is frozen.

The planting and treatment of the lower layer has brought about a change to this garden – from a natural, relaxed style to a clearly defined one. Many elements in the lower layer are responsible, among them and possibly the most important is the way the grass is grown and tended.

Grass and Grasses

Grass is foliage. It is there all the year round and its use is one of the most fundamental factors in all gardens except those from which it is excluded. It is so often the starting point of the garden design, around which everything else must fit, and yet its essential role in the foliage features of the garden is hardly ever mentioned or even recognised.

The colour and texture of the lawn is influenced by factors other than the purely aesthetic. Both the climate and the amount of wear the lawn receives will determine the choice of composition of grasses. It is no good expecting billiard-table perfection in a household whose members enjoy ball games. High rainfall areas will encourage the use of tough, wiry grasses, while cool-temperate gardens will be furnished with fine fescues with an admixture of ryegrass to taste. Climates with hot summers suggest the bermudas and St Augustines, some of which are of a soft blue that opens up a new range of compositional possibilities.

The role of lawns and hedges

The lower layer is not separate from the others and should be part of the overall picture. Nevertheless, special factors apply to it (not the least of which is its horizontality) and it is perhaps the greatest challenge to the garden designer who seeks to integrate all three layers.

In general, the role of the lawn in composition and design is related to its shape. If it is kept neat and its edges trimmed, it is unlikely to interfere with the design of the middle and upper layers. Our editorial eye takes account of its artificiality because we know that we are in a garden. In fact, the wild garden with its long grass and tall flowers needs to be created with great artfulness if we are not to see it as plain unkempt. If we know we are in open country we allow for that and see beauty where, in a cultivated environment, we would only sense neglect.

A lawn can be made to appear to lose its boundaries where it meets the woody denizens of the higher layers in several ways. Perhaps the simplest of these is to make it border on to a planting of dwarf shrubs, such as Japanese azaleas, slow-growing conifers, or *Cistus*, which then graduate upwards towards taller shrubs behind. In this way, the lower and middle layers merge imperceptibly, just as the middle and upper ones do.

ABOVE Glyceria maxima *'Variegata' grows to its full 1.2m/4ft height in moist, rich soils. This grass has arching leaves boldly striped with deep cream, and its spring shoots bear a distinctly pink tinge.*

Another idea is to use the theme of grasses themselves, so that the lawn becomes, at its extremity, a series of mown curves among clumps of specimen grasses. The first ones to be encountered would be the fescues such as *Festuca glauca*, whose smoky-blue hummocks, only centimetres high, associate perfectly with *F. amethystina*, a taller cousin of 30cm/12in in height or a little more and of a grey that has lilac and violet in it. Beyond these, sedges such as *Carex trifida* could be made to carry on the grey theme up to 60cm/24in, with the 1.2m/4ft, brilliantly blue-grey *Helictotrichon sempervirens* leading the eye to the foliage of the conical-columnar conifer *Chamaecyparis lawsoniana* 'Pembury Blue'. Variations on such themes are legion, but attention needs to be paid to the question of sun and shade. A sun-facing garden with a brake of trees and shrubs at its further boundary will not lend itself to plantings such as the one above, which depends upon sun, as the trees will cast shade. Here, every effort should be made to avoid dryness and to encourage conditions that will allow the lawn gradually to merge with woodland plantings.

RIGHT *Grass is the fundamental lower-layer feature of many gardens. Here it is used in several subtle ways. The curves outlined in mown grass lend shape and continuity to the shrubs and trees on the right; the flowers growing in the longer grass give a meadow-like feel to the scene. The mown grass makes the garden seem longer.*

Rheum species are lower-layer plants whose large, lush leaves suggest coolness and calm. Their tall, flowering stems erupt into the middle layer exuberantly, but their foliage remains closely related to nearby lower-layer neighbours.

Of course, the middle layer does not meet the lower one only at the garden's periphery. To give the impression that it does would be an oversimplification. The middle layer may have components right out in the middle of the garden as lawn specimens or as members of the plant communities that make up mixed borders in island form.

Like the lawn, a hedge is made of plants that are grown primarily for their foliage. Together with the lowly grasses that we often fail to think of as 'plants' at all, hedges turn the garden into an arena of green. Whether within or bounding the garden, hedges act as a foil for the flowers. They are, too, features in which texture, weave and nap are as worthy of thought and choice as anything else.

There is a great deal of difference in style and mood between a close-clipped hedge of yew, symmetrical and formal and yet the perfect background for the bouffant extravagances of a herbaceous border, and one composed of *Cotoneaster darwinii*, whose prickly informal dress demands the discipline of shrubs among the summer flowers.

The melting together of the layers is important wherever it looks natural. This will usually be at the periphery, but will not always be so. Elsewhere, the fact that a garden is an artificial environment must be allowed and lines of demarcation permitted to be drawn. The firm line of a well-trimmed lawn-edge is extremely attractive and its use in the same garden as a disguised boundary for the lawn suggests an understanding of the lawn as both foliage and a sort of outdoor carpet.

MERGING THE LOWER AND MIDDLE LAYERS

The advent of the mixed border has been a great blessing. Shrubs and herbaceous perennials that once were separated into their own quarters now coexist, and we no longer have to face the Cold with tracts of bare soil which lie there nakedly awaiting a blanket of snow. The middle layer meets the lower one more frequently and is represented in parts of the garden from which it was previously absent. Much more interplay is, therefore, possible, and the lower layer has more chances to be less of a discrete garden floor. Often, this meeting occurs between shrubs of statures that fit into the layers so perfectly that this form of categorisation is shown for the formalised exercise it is; frequently, too, the shrubs meet both herbaceous perennials and flower-bearing annuals.

There is happy confusion of the layers, such as when the flower spikes of the taller perennials tower above the shorter shrubs. For all their summer height they are still creatures of ground level. For the most part that is where their foliage occurs, and their tallness is short-lived. Amid the riot of flower colour that erupts in the garden in the Warm, foliage in the lower layer has a tougher job making an impact than it has higher up. The foliage of herbaceous perennials can never be taken as a permanent feature in the garden, either. It is gone for much of the year and its absence must not destroy the harmony of the garden.

LARGE-LEAVED PERENNIALS

Everything should be done to maximise the impact of all perennials whose foliage is dramatic, bold or conspicuous. They should never have other plants placed in front of them, even if it means having larger plants at the front in some places. The rule about small things being planted in front of large is one that, like so many other 'laws' of gardening, should be ignored. Scale can be preserved by backing such plants with other large ones. This gives a feeling of undulation to a border or bed; a pleasing irregularity that is in keeping with today's less geometrical approach to garden design.

ABOVE Ornamental rhubarbs are noble additions to the lower layer and not to be spoken of in the same breath as Rheum rhaponticum, *the culinary rhubarb. Varieties with purple undersides to the leaves –* R. palmatum *'Atrosanguineum' or* R.p. *'Bowles's Variety' are the ones to look for, as is* R.p. *var.* tanguticum, *which is purple-tinted on both leaf surfaces.*

LEFT Bergenias are conspicuous in the lower layer. They are evergreen, and many of them become brownish-red or bronze-tinted in winter.

Kirengeshoma palmata is possessed of an elegance and enough aristocratic élan to make it stand out in a crowd. It is a waste of its talents to allow it to be hidden from view even in part; its neighbours should be those that shuffle up behind it, pushing it forward as if it were too modest to do so for itself. Its foliage will pay its rent for the most part, as it does not flower until summer is over, but the pale lemony flowers are delightful and go well with blue agapanthus or with late-flowering aconitums.

On the other hand, isolation suits *Crambe cordifolia* – not the solitary confinement that a lawn tree is subjected to, but the placing of other plants at a respectable distance. Its piles of large, broad leaves are not particularly noteworthy contenders in the beauty stakes, but they are certainly to be encouraged in the larger garden.

Moisture-loving perennials

Really big leaves with a boldness that comes from their being simple or from their compound components being large are often happiest near water or in rich soils which are always moist.

Rodgersias have compound leaves which, because they grow in dense masses, have the solidity of simple ones. These are superb plants, making thickets of 30cm/12in wide leaves about 76cm/30in high. The leaves congregate to make a *testudo* – a rippling shell of metallic bronze that matures to green briefly before turning to copper-bronze for most of the summer. To describe them thus is to exclude *R. tabularis*, which is distinct because of its simple leaves and their light green colour. It should be included in any garden where it can be grown, as its leaves are almost circular and 1m/3ft across, spreading parasol-like from the centrally-inserted stalks. It is a bit like a smaller-scale *Gunnera manicata* and can be used in gardens which are not large enough for the gunnera.

The flowers of rodgersias are rather like those of astilbes or filipendulas and are borne in feathery inflorescences well above the leaves. They may be cream or pink, but in either case are a distraction. Unlike the flowers of so many plants, they do not complement and enhance their own foliage, rather seeming to diminish it by being out of place. Perhaps the problem is that they seldom flower profusely and the lush generosity of the foliage sits unhappily with the few, incongruous flower-spikes. Some people cut them down or do not let them develop and one can see why.

There are about four other species of rodgersia and several hybrids. It is as well to obtain plants that you like rather than to try to be too exact about finding such and such a species. Sturdiness and good leaf colour with a sheen like that on oiled, suntanned skins is worth more than a correct label.

Those who want large, rounded leaves near water but also want flowers that counted might be tempted to grow species of *Petasites*, whose short flower-heads come in winter and bring a scent not

Epimediums may display tinted leaves in autumn or winter, and in some species the new shoots are also coloured. They prefer cool positions in partial shade, where they will flower well in spring. Those who wish to see the flowers at their best must steel themselves to cut off the foliage in late winter.

unlike cooked fruit. They should be warned that these plants tend to be insistently invasive, capable of sweeping down upon the civilised inhabitants of the garden like botanical Genghis Khans. They are well-loved by the sort of landscape architects who present their accounts and then leave town, but nobody should be fooled.

Peltiphyllum peltatum, by contrast, is a well-behaved plant which has a soil-binding rhizomatous mat, above which coral-pink heads of saxifrage-like flowers appear in early spring on stalks about 60cm/24in high. Later, the flowers are replaced by 30cm/12in wide, perfectly round leaves, much like smaller versions of those of *Rodgersia tabularis*. This is an excellent plant and is one that is in character when growing with *Meconopsis* and candelabra primulas.

Veratrum nigrum is a shade-lover and another happy inhabitant of watery neighbourhoods. It has been rare for a long time but is now becoming readily available, so that its exquisitely pleated, fan-shaped leaves are recognised by more and more gardeners. These leaves are among the most beautiful and I will never forget my first sight of their simple dark-greenness, belied by the subtlety of their form. The leaves are enough; the feathery eruptions of small, dark red flowers are a bonus.

Versatile hostas

When one thinks of perennials with fine foliage that associate with water, hostas soon come to the fore, but they need not be confined to the waterside. Indeed, hostas will thrive in any part of the garden that is not too hot or sunny and where the soil is rich and does not become dry in the summer. The richer and moister the soil, the more sun they can take, so that they can be seen in some gardens in positions that might be thought to be too hot for them. These are likely to be the gardens of experienced plantsmen; it is as well to get to

LEFT ABOVE Rodgersia pinnata *is one of the best of its species for flowering. There is a white form but the creamy pink of the usual form of the species is more desirable.*

LEFT BELOW *Ligularias are plants for moist, rich soils and sunny positions. The leaves of several species are prized for their rich mahogany reverses.*

know hostas gradually by trying the different kinds in shady places and graduating to sunnier ones as experience increases.

There are several groups of plants whose names are in a state of confusion, but the hostas must be the worst. It is likely that the hosta you pick up in a garden centre will be wrongly named or labelled with such convoluted 'Latin' names that you will not wish to be bothered. Do not despair. If a hosta appeals to you because of its leaves buy it, and let the name get sorted out at a later date.

Hostas – ignoring for a moment their flowers – fall into two main kinds; those with plain leaves and those whose leaves are variegated. The plain-leaved kinds may be green, as in most forms of *Hosta fortunei* and in other species such as *H. plantaginea*. Others are glaucous, which is to say that they have a pronounced blue-grey tint to their leaves. Perhaps the best of these is the superb *H. sieboldiana* var. *elegans*, whose leaves are the largest among hostas. They can be over 30cm/12in wide and are beautifully blue with a pearly-grey overtone. The flowers are rather disappointing, but this is one of the best of all foliage plants among herbaceous perennials.

Variegated hostas come in all shapes and sizes. The leaves may be green with white edges, green with cream or yellow borders, or variegated so that the green is at the margin of the leaf. In some varieties the leaves are undulate and may be strongly variegated as well. They vary in size from dwarf plants to large, cabbagey ones and rather than suggest some of the many varieties, I advise you to look at some in full leaf and see what you would like to have in your garden.

The flowers of most hostas are quite beautiful and look like white or mauve lilies. Unlike those of rodgersias, they manage to look appropriate, but there are many people who would not agree and who would wish that they did not flower.

Hostas can easily cause collector's mania. Anything that comes in great variety and gives rise to a steady stream of new varieties will do this, and it is a pity, as the glory of hostas is that they do so much for their neighbours and themselves look all the better for being in company. A monoculture of hostas is a bore. The solid leaves of hostas contrast beautifully with the featheriness of ferns, and the

ABOVE *Although they may be recommended for shade, a rich moist soil will support a population of plants even where sun reaches them.* Hosta sieboldiana *var.* elegans *associates evocatively with the fronds of the shuttlecock fern,* Matteuccia struthiopteris *and with the flowers of candelabra primulas.*

LEFT Hosta fortunei *'Marginato-Alba' is the most luxurious of the white-margined hostas. Like almost all plants variegated with white or cream, it needs more shade than those with yellow variegation, otherwise it will burn. Hostas with blue-grey leaves or golden variegation will take a great deal of sun as long as the soil is rich and deep and does not dry out.*

cool colours of primulas seem to make their leaves look even more stately. Nestled at the feet of rhododendrons and tucked cosily into a peaty soil, they make the perfect statement about the strength of the lower layer. It is not a dumping-ground for dubious things called 'ground cover' or 'space-fillers'. It is a part of the garden in which the successful use of foliage can bring the richest rewards and tax the most fertile imaginations.

Perennials for Shady Positions

The borage family provides one of the best ground-level plants for shady situations. *Pulmonaria saccharata* is often referred to as a 'ground-cover' plant, but this is an anti-gardening term. To describe it as a plant that covers the ground is to make a distinction with a difference, as the emphasis is on the plant and not on the ground. This is one of the lungworts, so called because of the spotting on their leaves which reminded herbalists of the texture of a lung. The doctrine of analagous healing led them to use it to treat lung conditions – no doubt with as little success as the gardener who grows it in full sun on a sandy soil. This species demonstrates better than the others the unusual, blotched leaves with their patches of grey, and indeed is so variegated that many leaves will appear to be almost wholly grey.

In contrast to the much larger symphytum, the blue flowers of *P. saccharata*, arising from pink buds, are a great asset to the plant and are something that one is drawn to look for in the spring. 'Margery Fish' is a relatively new variety that appears better than the older ones, while forms with even better flowers are coming to the fore.

Opinions vary greatly on the merits of the flowers of Solomon's seal. Some would say that the plant (whatever it might be, and that is far from certain, as we shall see in a moment) is best grown for its foliage alone, while others dote on the flowers. I think that it is much like any other good shade-tolerant plant; its foliage is excellent in the less formal parts of the garden, and its flowers are attractive while they last. The variegated forms (whatever *they* might be) are plants that I would be very careful about. The very best forms have flowers that do nothing for the foliage at all, and it is really for the foliage that you will have chosen them. They tend to be weak in constitution and are regarded by slugs as a sort of over-appetising starter; they eat so much that they have no room for the main course.

Pulmonaria saccharata *varies considerably in the degree of spotting on its leaves. Many gardeners prize forms which are almost completely grey, while others prefer the speckled effect because it contrasts so well with plain leaves. The association between large, simple leaves and small compound ones contributes to the benefit of both.*

Solomon's seal is *Polygonatum multiflorum* of gardens, but is really a hybrid between that species and *P. odoratum* and should be called *P.* × *hybridum*. Its variegated form will be found in nurseries as 'Variegatum' tacked on to either. This is markedly variegated with cream but is liable to disappear within a season of its being planted. Just to confuse the issue further, it sometimes appears as *P.* × *hybridum* 'Striatum'. All this is very complicated, but there is worse to come. Never mind. The purpose of the exercise is to unravel the knot that is locking up the identity of the good garden plant that is a variegated Solomon's seal. This is found as *P. japonicum* of gardens, in the form 'Variegatum'. Now, *P. japonicum* of gardens is a name which has been applied to four species at least, one or two of which are themselves riddled with synonymy. The current state of play is that you may find it also as *P. falcatum* 'Variegatum' and either name should yield up the right plant. It should not appear very strongly variegated, and if you have got your eye in for those variegations that look healthy and those that don't, then you should be able to tell it apart from the weaker *P.* × *hybridum* variety.

Everyone agrees that Solomon's seal and lily-of-the-valley go well together, particularly in shady, damp places. Both tolerate heavily lime-charged soils, too. To my mind, there is little point in mucking about with such a delightful combination, and I would grow the variegated Solomon's seal somewhere else. What I would never do is to try to persuade anyone that it is a good idea to grow it side-by-side with the variegated lily-of-the-valley. This is an excellent plant, whose flowers are as scented as the plain form, and its variegation is creamy yellow. Perhaps ferns, either feathery or strap-shaped, are the best sorts of foils for these two beauties. If you can obtain it, the pink-flowered lily-of-the-valley is, I think, entirely to be treasured, but others disagree. It has been consigned to the verbal compost heap by some authorities on taste as well as on plants, while others whose aesthetic and horticultural expertise is to be admired have extolled its delicate virtues. I see nothing wrong in growing it among the white ones and would not banish it to a solitary existence. By the same token, to make it compete with variegated plants would be to ask too much.

Both lily-of-the-valley and Solomon's seal have giant versions. *Convallaria majalis* 'Fortin's Giant' is the large version of the former and is bigger in all its parts, with wider leaves and flowers and with the useful habit of blooming about a week later than the rest. It will take quite a lot of sun – rather more than the species itself, although that can be spread out from the shady to the half-sunny and will flower over a longer period as a result. The giant Solomon's seal is – here we go again – *Polygonatum commutatum, P. giganteum*, or *P. canaliculatum*, depending on your point of view. In all fairness, you will usually find it under the middle name of those three, but it is unmistakable, as this species from the United States is twice as large as the European species (whatever that is).

Solomon's seal is the perfect link between foliage layers. In this inspired planting there is months-long interest provided by the contrast of leaf forms and by the evergreen Pieris *'Forest Flame' in the background. The artistry lies in the planning behind a deceptively natural scene.*

Maidenhair ferns sum up all that is delicate, fresh and delightful in the great fern family. Although Adiantium capillus-veneris *is small, its impact is great.*

Ferns for Moist or Dry Places

Ferns, which go with hostas like ham goes with eggs, are plants whose neglect as garden ornament defies understanding. At how many garden centres can you expect to find a range of hardy ferns? Perhaps there is still a reaction against those awful, depressing Victorian ferneries (monoculture again), but it seems improbable that such prejudice should linger for almost a century. It is more likely that the numbers of fern plants are insufficient to allow nurseries to build up enough stocks to list ferns. To raise them from spores is unlikely to be economic and, in any case, varieties of the species do not come true from spores.

One does not have to grow those ferns that have oddly-shaped fronds, been given strange names and propagated by division. The spores of many species can be obtained and, simply by growing them in sterilised soil and not allowing foreign spores to invade, enough plants may be grown to stock the quieter corners of even the largest gardens. The shuttlecock, or ostrich fern, *Matteuccia struthiopteris*, is the best possible neighbour for *Hosta sieboldiana* var. *elegans*. Its fresh green contrasts with the smoky blue of the hosta, and the upright, flaring shuttlecocks of filigreed fronds match the hosta for dignity while presenting a totally different style. It runs very gently, making a gradually increasing colony and providing offsets for removal to other parts of the garden.

The ordinary male ferns, *Dryopteris borreri* and the like, are by no means to be dismissed. They are evergreen, tough and carry on the fern theme through the Cold. The complete contrast between their dull green, pinnate fronds and the shiny, bright green, entire, strap-shaped ones of *Phyllitis scolopendrium*, the hart's tongue fern, is extremely effective all year round. Indeed, the hart's tongue stands alone as first-class, hardy and thoroughly delicious lower-level flora. There are several varieties which can be obtained from specialist nurseries or from fern enthusiasts. Most of these involve the fronds in varying degrees of cresting. This is very attractive, but it may also be thought that nothing can surpass the simplicity of

ABOVE Matteuccia struthiopteris *shows it is well-named the shuttlecock fern. It is also called the ostrich fern because of the imagined likeness of its feathery fronds to ostrich plumes. It is at its best by water or even in it, so long as it is planted shallowly enough that its crowns are not covered.*

LEFT *The rich, shiny green fronds of* Phyllitis scolopendrium, *the hart's tongue fern, are always ornamental; when they are unfurling, they are fascinating. It is an ideal companion for hostas with blue-grey leaves and a good foil for brightly-coloured polyanthus.*

The soft-shield fern is hardy and will grow well in dry conditions as well as moist – in fact it is happy almost anywhere. There are several good varieties of this evergreen, 1.2m/4ft fern in cultivation: this one is Polystichum setiferum *'Plumosum Divisilobum'*

the normal form, especially when multicoloured polyanthus are seen twinkling amid its unembellished glossiness.

Fern collecting is as addictive as any other sort and gets hold of people in a way that can mean that their gardens are reduced to having all the appeal of an expanse of chopped lettuce. Most fern species have whole lists of forms in which deformity becomes a quality almost beyond price and in which the bizarre is elevated to the height of chic. For the balanced garden, the impact of large, pinnate leaves and the value of fresh, rich greenery will be paramount.

Osmunda regalis, the royal fern, is one of the noblest of all plants and displays all that is best in large, pinnate leaves. The combination of grace and sheer size is irresistible, and it is one of that 'family' of plants that one thinks of whenever shady, moist places are mentioned – *Gunnera, Rodgersia, Hosta, Matteuccia* and so on. It is distinct from the shuttlecock fern, being nothing like as feathery, and for this reason the two can be planted near to one another to mutual advantage. The royal fern is extremely widespread in nature. It is native to Europe (including Britain) and to the United States, where it meets its congener, *O. cinnamomea* in moist, warm woods in the south-east. For all that, the second species is hardy in colder climates and, while its stature is not as imposing as that of *O. regalis*, its fronds are ravishing in spring when they unfurl to reveal their covering of creamy-brown, powdery down.

Although ferns rightly suggest moist, humid places, they are very adaptable. Although they are unlikely to reproduce *in situ* from spores in dry spots, they will often grow there. The toughest species are the male, shield and lady ferns. These give a cooling effect to a sunny slope and, although they will have to be watered assiduously until they are well established, they will eventually settle down and can be almost neglected.

Although by no means a large-leaved fern, *Polypodium vulgare*, the common polypody, is extremely effective for growing in the driest positions. Driest, that is to say, but for the air, which must be reasonably moisture-laden. In the village in which I live, there is an old smithy whose roof is covered with this fern. In hot weather, prolonged over some weeks, it becomes reduced to a charred mat but it soon recovers with the rains and returns to its cool, green self. In the garden here it decorates the forks of old oak trees, growing purely epiphytically, but it also has a lower-level role. On dry, stony banks where the sun does not strike – dry shade, the bane of all gardeners – the little polypody makes wide colonies for all the world as if it were lapping up a stream's bounty. How you are to obtain the plant I do not know. It seldom figures in nursery lists and is rarely seen in garden centres. Try though. It will be worth it.

Variegation: A Link Between Moist and Dry

Variegated plants with large leaves take most sun where they have most moisture, as do most other plants. It is as well to remember that there is a rough general rule about sun and kinds of variegation. If a leaf has a gold marginal variegation it is likely to take a lot of sun. If the gold occupies the main part of the centre of the leaf, the plant will require at least dappled shade. Plants with white marginal variegations tend to burn in sun, and those with white centres always do.

This rule applies to hostas, as well as to quite a wide range of other plants, including shrubs. Hostas with white in the leaf are in general not suitable for planting in sun, no matter how richly moist the soil. Such plants as *H. albomarginata, H. crispula* and *H. decorata*, all of which have white-margined leaves, will burn by midsummer, even though they bear the species name. *H.* 'Thomas Hogg' will take more sun than others, and may be told apart from them by the texture of the leaves, which is very smooth both above and below. All these names are currently in use but they have no real botanical standing.

The same rule applies to forms of *Brunnera macrophylla*. This is like a large-leaved forget-me-not. After it has flowered its leaves become even bigger and make a fine show of foliage near water, although it is a plant that can make the transition from a watery environment to a drier one, in this case provided that there is shade. There are several forms with variegated leaves, but care is needed to make sure that they do not burn in sun or in wind. 'Variegata' is an old variety, while a superbly cream-margined form called 'Hadspen Cream' is becoming more widely available. Perhaps the one that will tolerate most sun is 'Langtrees'. This is spotted and splashed with grey and seemed very happy in a most exposed position where I saw it beside a pond in a windswept garden.

Variegation in long, upright, grassy leaves is represented in some of the irises, among which *I. pseudacorus* 'Variegata' is pre-eminent for the moist, shady banks of ponds and streams and as a marginal plant. The leaves are green in late

LEFT Hosta *'Thomas Hogg' is the most tolerant of white-margined plants and is therefore the best for all-round garden use. Its foliage is notably smooth and fresh-looking.*

BELOW *The beautifully marked, large, heart-shaped leaves of* Brunnera macrophylla *'Variegata'. This plant must have shade, and is best in a moist soil or as a waterside subject. The forget-me-not flowers bloom in copious quantities on 46cm/18in stems, and are spring-borne. The foliage of a new form, 'Hadspen Cream', is less likely to scorch and is distinguished by broad cream borders to the leaves.*

summer, but until then they are beautifully and strikingly striped with yellow. The flowers are those of the common 'flag' iris, but are neatly marked with brown. This plant can react with another – *I. pallida* 'Variegata' – in marking the transition from the moister, shadier parts of the garden to the drier, sunnier ones. The second plant keeps its leaf colour until the leaves disappear in the autumn, and is one of the finest plants of all with upright, variegated leaves that can be grown in cool temperate gardens. There appear to be two forms, one of which is cream and the other more yellow in variegation. There seems little doubt that some differentiation in naming should be applied to them, but meanwhile, if you are ordering the plant, it is as well to be specific. Sun and a good, well-drained soil will suit either.

Phormiums in many different variegations have come into general cultivation in recent years. They, too, have upright, sword-shaped, or sometimes rather grassy foliage and are rather slow-growing. Some are small enough to qualify as lower-layer plants, but it is unfortunately true that these tend to be the least hardy. Phormiums such as 'Maori Sunrise' and 'Dazzler', in which there is a variegation involving quite bright reds, are only for gardens where there is very little frost. Yellow-variegated forms, such as 'Yellow Wave' are a lot hardier but will still take a ferocious beating where winters are cold. Too much continental cold (whatever the continent) will be too great a burden for them to bear. This warning is issued because the plants are so appealing and so beautiful that it is hard to resist them when they appear in the garden centres. No person with an eye for foliage can possibly fail to be smitten, but it is too easy to spend good money only to be disappointed.

With perennials, as with shrubs, it often happens that a plant that has beautifully variegated foliage will have flowers that are almost an embarrassment. They may be disproportionately small, or they may be of a colour that is unpleasant or hard to place. The strongest case for a magic spell that would abolish flowering in variegated plants is put by *Symphytum* × *uplandicum* 'Variegatum'. This is a comfrey that is not often seen but when it is is rarely forgotten. It is a strongly-growing plant, generally 90cm/36in tall, but I have seen it over 1.2m/4ft, with foliage of such a superb colouring that it is almost perfection. The leaves are a subtle grey-green and are blessed with broad, cream margins. It is too often grown in shade, where it reverts badly, but in sun it is less inclined to do so. The hybrid itself is notable for having flowers of the purest azure blue, even though they arise from pink buds, as do nearly all the comfreys and, for that matter, most of the family of borages, to which they belong. The variegated form can manage only the most undistinguished, wishy-washy mauve, which is an insult to the glory of the foliage. It is this sort of plant that gives the foliage-only school quivers for its bow.

In the case of *Phlox paniculata* 'Norah Leigh' it is easy to see why some people describe the flowers

A group of irises with variegated leaves is of the greatest value in establishing links between moist and dry soils. Forms of I. pseudacorus *thrive in wet soils, while* I. pallida *and its varieties prefer more dry conditions and revel in sun.*

Phormium 'Dazzler' is one of many new hybrids among the New Zealand flaxes, but must be considered tender in all but the most favoured gardens. It will stand severe frosts, but only for short periods.

as of little account, but it is also not difficult to work out that they are categorising the plant as a border phlox, rather than as a herbaceous plant with variegated leaves and lilac flowers. Should you attempt to put it with its peers – such phloxes as 'July Glow', whose rich, cherry pink is typical of the range of strong colours – it will be fine until they all flower, as its buff-cream variegation is very good indeed. Your first instinct upon seeing the flower clash would be to remove the blooms as soon as possible. Regard it as a plant in its own right, on the other hand, and you would place it somewhere else entirely, where its foliage could stand out among plain greens and where its flowers would be at a good distance from those that have been bred for show, rather than being as Nature intended.

Those who criticise *Phlox* 'Norah Leigh' do not seem to voice the same opinion about the variegated forms of *Fuchsia magellanica*. These are, of course, shrubs, but in garden terms they behave as perennials, being cut to the ground in most winters. Their flowers are much smaller than those of other hardy fuchsias – Mrs Popple' and 'Mme Cornelissen', for instance – and are minute in comparison with those of the greenhouse fuchsias. There are two kinds. *F.m.* 'Variegata' has a generous amount of small leaves, all margined with rich cream which is flushed with pink. *F.m.* 'Versicolor' is more subtle. It is of the same attractive, leafy habit, but each leaf is a soft grey-green, suffused with purplish pink. As the leaf matures it begins to show the margin of cream that is seen throughout in the other variety.

The flowers of both plants are a decoration and an asset to the leaves, and the plants are in perfect internal scale, as you would expect from something that has not been encouraged to be more than Nature intended. It would, however, be stupid to place them near fuchsias with larger flowers and thus subject them to unfair comparison. By an accident of planning, I have *F.m.* 'Versicolor' growing among old-fashioned roses. The foliage works well as a foil for that of the roses, and the flowers of the roses have, being old ones and devoid of the modern loud hues, something of the colours of the fuchsia leaves in them. The fuchsia flowers, though, are out of their class and I fear that I must try to do what I have been avoiding, which is to lift and move the very wide and well-established fuchsia thicket without disturbing the roses.

Not far away, *F.m.* var. *gracilis* – green-leaved and with long, exquisitely slender flowers – lives in perfect harmony with a colony of *Yucca recurvifolia*. The busy foliage of the fuchsia, apple-green and mobile, contrasts prettily with the long, grey, stationary straps of the yuccas. What is more, the yucca blooms, although much larger than those of the fuchsia, do not appear in any way to make an alien association, but in some mysterious way to complement them. The deep source of this compatibility lies in their both being unspoilt children of Nature, whatever else may be working in their favour.

Dryness and Grey-leaved Plants

Grey leaves usually mean that a plant is adapted to drought, wind, salt or a sharply drained soil. *Pulmonaria* is an exception, in that it prefers shade; *Hosta* is another, because it must have moisture; and *Anaphalis*, because it cannot withstand drought, is a third. Apart from these, it may be taken that a grey leaf on a plant of the lower layer, whether it be herbaceous or shrubby, can be grown in the hotter, drier parts of the garden.

Anaphalis is represented in gardens by several species, all of which make mounds of grey foliage. The flowers are white everlastings in tight clusters (reminiscent of those of some *Achillea* species). The advantage of the genus is that its members can provide grey in places where other grey-leaved plants might not thrive because, although they will take sun if the soil is moist, they will also do well in shade provided that they are not dripped on by trees.

Achillea has species that have either green or grey leaves, while a few are somewhere in between. In general, they are on the way to being drought-resistant and true heat-lovers, but share with *Anaphalis* a liking for moisture-retentive soils, while not giving up the ghost in a drought in quite such a hopeless manner. Most of the species and varieties have feathery leaves, as opposed to the simple ones of *Anaphalis*, and some are among the front rank of grey-leaved plants.

Nowadays there is more emphasis on the

An emphasis on grey rather than white foliage gives a clean, fresh look to this Mediterranean-style planting. Artemisias, hellebores, achilleas and other grey, grey-green and aromatic plants are all suited to an arrangement that can be left to itself in the driest weather.

flowers of achilleas and less on their foliage. There is nothing wrong with this; in fact the new Galaxy achilleas are among the most lovely of herbaceous plants. It is just a pity that one or two species of outstanding foliage beauty have fallen into neglect. *A. grandifolia* is one that is not often seen now, and it is to be hoped that its filigreed, deeply cut foliage will come back into favour. It is very grey, and its small white flowers do not detract from its leafy attractiveness. Much more often grown is 'Moonshine', whose flat heads of flowers are bright yellow and whose foliage is, again, feathery and grey, but this time a little more on the green side.

Artemisias are the ultimate in grey filigree and among them *A. arborescens* is the most delicately lacy. Technically it is a shrub, but it is cut to the ground in most places by hard frost, to make fresh growth the following year. Indeed, where it overwinters in its shrubby mode, it should be cut back with secateurs in the spring to encourage a profuse onrush of foliage.

All these grey plants benefit by association with their own kind or with things that contrast strongly with them. Sometimes an inspired combination of flowers and foliage can happen by accident. I have *Artemisia arborescens* displaying its candy-floss froth of silvery grey among the flowers of large-flowered, tender fuchsias that overwinter outside where I live. It is one of the happiest and most unlikely plant associations I have ever seen. I really must try Graham Stuart Thomas's suggestion of planting it with *Nerine bowdenii*.

Perhaps the best and most showily effective of the artemisias is *A. ludoviciana* var. *latiloba*. This is almost as white in its leaf as *Senecio cineraria* and has similarly jagged, lobed leaves. It is about 60cm/24in tall or less and I have seen it in some combinations with other plants that owed everything to serendipity. In one garden it was among many plants of *Alchemilla mollis*, which formed a grey-green carpet for the half-dozen, shining white achilleas. After a shower of rain the shimmering jewels of the drops caught up in the hairs of the alchemilla leaves were sheer magic in company with the purity of the much larger senecio leaves. The alchemillas were self-sown seedlings, and this goes to show that what happens best often happens by luck. It is those who do not observe and gain from such things that are the losers.

Grey, silver and white foliage

I am not a lover of colour schemes or 'themes', as I find them to be restrictive, taking little account of the characteristics of a plant other than its colour. Those schemes which use white and grey to make so-called white gardens often fail, in my opinion, and prove a truism that holds good throughout ornamental horticulture: wherever a contrast is made, the characteristics being contrasted will appear to be exaggerated or reinforced. We have seen throughout this book examples in which light green, dark green, gold, copper, and all kinds of other characteristics of foliage have been seen more clearly because they have been contrasted one with another. These distinctions and comparisons work because there are no absolutes, no perfect degree of light greenness or of copper tone, for instance, against which others would show up as imperfect and undesirable.

White, however, is a different matter. White is white, the test of purity and cleanness. While it may be juxtaposed with black (the pure absence of colour) and offends no eye when seen neutrally against the colours (all of which make up white), it

New Zealand's natural conditions often favour grey-leaved plants. Among them are the senecios, and Senecio greyi *of gardens (the true species is tender) will tolerate cold conditions, drought and maritime exposure.*

cannot allow anything that is merely an impure version of itself to be seen as anything but unclean. Grey, therefore, when seen against white, appears to be merely dirty. Once again, the distinction has to be made between grey and blue. Blue will go very well with white and plants are often described as having grey foliage when it is really blue.

White flowers play no part in all this, but stand out on their own. Our eye allows for the variety of tones in grey foliage and accepts that white flowers associate perfectly well with it. Where flower whiteness is brought into the calculations of the eye is where it is less than pure and becomes grey-looking. For example, the New Zealand daisy-bush, *Olearia macrodonta*, looks most decorative when its holly-like, light grey leaves are allowed to play their part unalloyed in the foliage scene. Its flowers are in large clusters of lawn-sized daisies, but are of a really dingy off-white. While they hang there, the shrub has all the appearance of needing a wash.

Olearia × scilloniensis, on the other hand, has flowers of the purest white. Its leaves are not of nearly such a distinguished grey, and yet the plant looks as clean as a whistle when in flower. Similarly, *Anaphalis triplinervis* has leaves of a much better grey than those of *A. yedoensis*, so that it looks the better plant while not in flower. Flowering, though, reveals large, nicely white heads on the latter species, while the former looks as though someone had emptied the vacuum cleaner over it.

The white garden works well if all its greys are blue and all its whites – including those of the flowers – are truly white. Unfortunately this is rarely so and those unfortunate denizens that fail to achieve a vestal degree of purity lend an unforgivable air of slumminess. Of course, there have been successful and beautiful all-white gardens – Vita Sackville-West's garden at Sissinghurst springs to mind – but these have been the handiwork of gardeners of rare genius, and we lesser mortals can rarely duplicate the effect. We will have to admit that grey and white are often mutually deleterious, and that the elements of a 'white' garden should be dispersed to those parts of the garden where each can do the most good.

Romneya coulteri, the Californian tree poppy, is strictly speaking a sub-shrub, but often behaves as a herbaceous plant where winters are less than mild. It can grow to 1.8m/6ft and often does, although it is usually about 1.2m/4ft tall. A plant of this size, with brightly silver, lush and prettily-divided foliage, is a force to be reckoned with in the garden. Its great, crinkled, white poppy-flowers ensure it a place in the garden aristocracy. What heresy to consign this beauty to the tawdry *salon* that is the 'white' garden! How much better to allow it to make relationships in its own right with other plants. Its leaves might echo the frilliness of those of the tree peonies, the silveriness of *Cytisus battandieri*, or be highlighted by a backing of dark green myrtle.

Some genera spring readily to mind when 'grey' is mentioned, and none more so than *Salvia*. Unfortunately, although salvias are plants in which there is a great deal of interest, it is hard to avoid the feeling that that interest is likely to be short-lived. After some years of looking after the British National Collection of the genus, I am forced to the opinion that they are, for the most part, unsatisfactory garden plants. Few have foliage that is really attractive, and the ones that do have nearly all got green leaves. They also have ungainly habits and tend to sprawl over

Stachys olympica *is an excellent silvery carpet which is only slightly marred by its small, reddish-purple flowers. 'Silver Carpet' has flowers that fail to develop, leaving the foliage unblemished. It grows well in full sun and thrives in the driest places. It is an excellent foil for long, linear leaves like those of* Hemerocallis *and* Sisyrinchium striatum *and can sometimes be seen beneath old-fashioned roses.*

anything that happens to be near. What is more, those that are extolled as 'foliage' plants tend to be extremely disappointing.

Salvia argentea is a biennial or short-lived perennial whose flat rosettes of woolly leaves are the nearest thing to angora that the open garden can sustain. Unfortunately, they are beloved of slugs and soon lose their charm when full of holes and besmirched by rain-splashed soil. By autumn they are likely to be as attractive as last week's football socks. If salvias are grown as plants whose flowers are, with a few exceptions, gorgeous, beautifully shaped, vivid and valuable because so many of them appear very late in the year, then they will be better understood. The vogue for thinking of them as plants noble in form and foliage is mistaken. Many do have lovely leaves, but they are short-lived, few are hardy, and their straggly habits rule them out for any role but that of flower-bearers.

Grey and grasses go together with more justification, but remember that many of these 'greys' are really blues. Blue grasses are found in the wild where conditions are dry, and should be afforded positions in the garden that they will enjoy. *Helictotrichon sempervirens*, also known as *Avena candida*, is a non-invasive, small grass which associates well with plants that like the same sorts of sunny locations. The clumps of bright, blue-grey leaves are topped with grey plumes and the plant is an ideal companion for such things as the border sedums, whose winey reds and deep maroons are present at the same time as the flower stems of the grass. *Elymus arenarius* has been praised by gardening writers over the years but really only deserves mention as one of the worst thugs that can be introduced to the garden. It is not unlike *Helictotrichon* to look at, although its leaves are broader, but it is as dangerous as the other is safe.

Shrubs in the Lower Layer

The herbaceous plants are by no means alone in lending to the garden the valuable greys and silvers. Possibly the best of all the lower layer silver-leaved plants is the incomparable *Convolvulus cneorum*. This is a truly wonderful plant, whose rolled-silver leaves can be seen shining in gardens where winters can be bitter and where freezing winds whip against its uncovered branches. The secret is to provide a sharply-drained soil not overwhelmed by nutrients where it will receive all the sun that it possibly can. It is a superb example of the combination of white flowers and silver leaves; the blooms are large and trumpet-shaped and keep coming when you think the plant must have overdone it. Planted with things of similar stature, like *Ceanothus* 'Blue Mound', and with plants that like a similar environment, such as the yellow-grey leaved *Phlomis* species, a maquis-like community can be built up in which fascinating associations are made on a small scale.

Convolvulus cneorum *is recommended generally for its spring flowering. In fact, when happily sited in a well-drained soil in full sun, it flowers almost all the year round, producing its largesse in the shape of large, ice-white trumpets on beds of pure, glossy silver. Among silver-leaved plants of small stature it has no peer and is far hardier than usually supposed as long as the drainage is impeccable.*

No plant, no matter how small, is insignificant in the foliage picture merely because of its size. Whereas the largest trees will be of no account if their leaves are drab and dull, a tiny, domed alpine will be mightily effective in the right place. In the dry community above, the rounded buns of the grey-leaved *Euryops acraeus*, a South African mountain plant with long-lasting yellow daisies, will be telling indeed, as will the hard, spiny cushions of *Dianthus erinaceus*.

Foliage combinations in which small shrubs occur can be of totally different kinds, even within the boundaries of a small garden. Some may be complicated, relying for their success on a combination of many elements, while others may be remarkable for their simplicity. I have described one example of brilliant foliage association on a tiny scale from the garden of Geoff Hamilton. Another, just a subtle, but even simpler, involved just one shrub and a small-leaved, creeping, evergreen lamium.

The shrub was *Pieris japonica* 'Variegata'. This is, even for the variegated form of a shrub, extraordinarily stunted in comparison with the green-leaved species, and yet it is in proportion with itself and looks in no way unhealthy. It forms a humpy, compact plant with tightly-packed foliage; each leaf has a green centre and a broad, yellow edge which is enough to reduce the green to a narrow band. When planted it seemed to float on a small sea of lamium. This is a plant that is recommended for 'ground cover' and it was certainly covering the ground, but it was as a foil for the pieris that it was performing to perfection. Each small leaf, as tightly-placed amid its neighbours as any on the pieris, was silver and green, but with the pattern reversed: a very narrow, dark green margin outlined the quite broad, silver centre.

One might be forgiven for being thought a little eccentric by lovers of 'foliage' plants. After all, whoever heard of someone being dumbstruck by a common dead nettle and a shrub that is really not all that distinguished? The point is that the right association of plants can raise the individual elements to heights that they could never achieve on their own. Gardening with foliage is almost always portrayed as something rather grand, to which only the cognoscenti can aspire. Examples such as these, in which little plants are used in simple ways to make beautiful pictures, should encourage the owners of the smallest gardens and the possessors of the shallowest pockets in their quest for gardening excellence.

Evergreen shrubs of the garden ground floor

Small, evergreen shrubs play a large part in the Cold, when gardens can become uninteresting at ground level if too much reliance is placed on herbaceous plants. Brightly coloured twigs and interesting shapes of deciduous woody plants are vital, of course, but low-growing, shrubby foliage, especially if it displays some colouring other than plain green, is a great asset to the winter garden. Little, shrubby forms of *Euonymus radicans* are

Euonymus fortunei *'Sunshine' will grow anywhere and is not daunted by poor soils, drought or neglect. In the lower layer it and its close relatives have many uses and may be allowed to grow round the stems of climbing plants or the pedestals of urns.*

extremely useful. This is not their correct designation, as they are, strictly, *E. fortunei* 'Variegatus'. They will be found as *E. radicans* 'Variegatus', and with cultivar names like 'Emerald and Gold', which is what it sounds like. 'Emerald Gaiety' is another. They are all bright little shrubs and have the supreme advantage of being absolutely bone hardy, so that they will grow where even ivy cannot. Indeed, they can change their habit dramatically and climb walls like ivy; when they latch on to trees they are just as difficult to dislodge.

Hardiness is not a well-known virtue of the hebes. In fact, once you have grown a good many of them it becomes more and more difficult to find any virtues in them that compensate for their boring regularity of structure. Nevertheless, there are one or two that are sufficiently hardy to be valuable as evergreen foliage items at the lower level, especially in the winter. *H. pinguifolia* 'Pagei' is small and blue-grey. *H. rakaiensis* is larger, bean-bag-shaped and green. Although hebes are nearly all evergreen and some have what might to some eyes be attractive purple tints in their leaves, I do not like them and will say no more about them lest I offend those who do.

Dwarf conifers and heathers associate very well. Abies procera *'Glauca Prostrata' has bristly, blue-grey foliage that is shown off by the gold of* Erica carnea *'Foxhollow' – the advantage is mutual all the year round.*

Dwarf and more prostrate conifers can be exciting if they are used properly and perfectly terrible if they are not. The secret is to mix the compact with the open, the prostrate with the rounded or upright, and green with other colours. To stick them in like candles on a birthday cake is not the most aesthetically pleasing arrangement. There is nothing at all wrong – in fact everything right – in allowing the dwarf ones (although few are really dwarf) to associate with those that are merely slow-growing, and those in their turn with the large ones, but the lower layer is the place for conifers that attain nothing much in terms of height. There are, of course, dozens, if not hundreds of them, but it would not be profitable to catalogue them here. The principle of their use – that each should relate to as many of its neighbours as possible in respect of some aspect of its character – is all that needs to be emphasised.

One or two, however, have caught the eye recently and look like being excellent garden plants. *Tsuga canadensis* 'Jeddeloh' is a flat bun-shaped version of the Canadian hemlock, only about 46cm/18in high, with branches that are a little pendulous. It is a good, fresh green even in the depth of winter. In striking contrast, *Abies procera* 'Glauca Prostrata', an old variety from the end of the last century, is typical of the prostrate, blue-grey, stiffly-branched conifers which complement the more densely-structured, green plants. *Juniperus squamata* 'Holger' is nest-shaped, with terminal branchlets that are slender and drooping, and with compact foliage that is yellow-green. Add a dash of *Iris reticulata* for late winter colour, some dwarf daffodils to follow and the marbled leaves of *Cyclamen hederifolium* to see the spring and summer through until they flower in autumn, and what more could you ask in the tiniest garden anywhere?

Heathers and their Companions

The shrubby element of the lower layer is by no means confined to dwarf shrubs. Many much taller plants whose bodies, as it were, are in the middle or even the upper layers will have their feet in the lower and form an important part of it. So it is desirable to plan related plantings to take account of this: what lies beneath the skirts of a taller shrub should be regarded as equally important to that which is related to it higher up. *Physocarpus opulifolius* 'Dart's Gold', for instance, clothes itself in bright, golden-yellow leaves right down to the ground, especially when it is young, and it is no bad idea to allow the gold to continue to spill over the ground by letting it be carried on by heathers such as *Calluna vulgaris* 'Beoley Gold' or, if a touch of old gold is wanted, *C.v.* 'Robert Chapman'.

This physocarpus is sometimes suggested as a companion for purple-leaved plants, an effect not difficult to achieve if 'purple' is taken with the usual pinch of salt, but the result can be truly awful. The association is much better if merely hinted at by employing, say, *Erica carnea* 'Vivellii', whose dense, needle-like foliage is bronzy-green in the Warm and red-bronze in the Cold. The physocarpus will have lost its leaves when the heath's colour deepens, but the gardener will have the relationship in his memory and it will provide a ghost of gold during the cold months.

Heathers are a great asset for plants whose roots neither accept competition nor tolerate dryness and heat. The eucryphias, bearers of white flowers in the very late summer which play the equivalent role to that of magnolias in spring, share with that genus a hatred of substrate competition and threat to their root systems. To grow heathers right up to their skirts (I can think of no better description, repetitious though it might be) is to do them a great favour, as the lesser plants are shallow-rooting and provide the coolest possible run for the deeper roots of the eucryphias. In such a case, the rich, dark, olive greens that the eucryphias exhibit may be carried on in the foliage of the heathers, and the heathers will shade over time into silvers and golds that will themselves find echoes elsewhere in the garden.

This use of heathers is greatly superior to the rather banal heather-and-conifer garden one sees so often. While using foliage to its ultimate degree, the heather-and-conifer garden only works well in a semi-wild setting and on a large scale, so that casual grass paths may wander through it like the tracks made by persistent sheep, and where no sharp boundaries of concrete, tarmac, gravel or hedges intrude. It might be thought that the heathers alone could serve as the lower layer of foliage; so they could, but at what a cost in sheer ennui! It is much better to use them sparingly, allowing them to end gracefully where something else begins, perhaps prompted by a change in level or of aspect, or by the intrusion of an uncrossable barrier like a large rock or the last seepings of the marginal area around a pond.

Heathers and conifers on an altogether larger scale. Nature seems to have been the only designer here; this planting demonstrates a sensitive understanding of flowers, foliage and site.

Integrating Lower-layer Garden Features

Plants that grow in water make some of the most lush features of the lowest layer of foliage. Apart from water-lilies, and others whose leaves float flatly, they tend to follow the precept that the wetter the place, the larger the leaves. Because plants are categorised and slotted into files marked 'water plant', 'marginal' or 'border plant', all too often the area immediately around a pond or other water feature stands in isolation from the rest of the garden. The water plants are put in baskets and submerged. A margin is created beside a pond or stream and its muddy shallows are planted up with marginals. Beyond that will be lawn or paths and this feature will have run out of steam and come to an abrupt end.

Water features are not the only ones that tend to become isolated, cut off from everything else in the garden by a *cordon sanitaire* created by a lack of creativity. The inability to integrate such features as rock and peat gardens into their surroundings, seen as often in large gardens as in small ones, is a pity as these special plantings can be brought into harmony with the rest of the garden quite easily by looking at the many ways in which foliage can be used to make links – a shape answering another, a patch of variegation linked to one further away. Devices such as these will help you avoid having a feature that looks like something all dressed up and nowhere to go.

Harmonious water plantings

In a natural design, plants follow a gradation from those that like to be up to their necks in water, through those that are happier to be clear of it in winter, to plants that enjoy a moist, humid environment but eschew contact with the water itself. You will find that a water planting will seem the most to-be-expected feature in the world if plants are arranged as they are in Nature. It will not be so oasis-like that good plantings in the rest of the garden look sparse and drought-stricken by comparison.

In the water you will, of course, wish to combine the reflective qualities of its surface with the coolness of the leaves of water-lilies and water hawthorn. There is little that can surpass the magic of their placid, green discs on a hot day, rocking just a trifle under the influence of a trickle of water. Rising above them, the 20cm/8in long, arrow-head leaves of *Sagittaria sagittifolia* make an interesting and bold contrasting shape and, with the white flowers above them, reflect beautifully on the clear surface of the water. The double-flowered form is superb; care should be taken to plant it a little more shallowly than the single – about 10cm/4in deep.

The range of marginals is great. Foliage varies from the long, thin and reedy, such as that of *Acorus calamus* – the sweet-scented rush, whose form 'Variegatus' is one of the loveliest – to the rounded, such as that of the marsh marigold. Grassy types of leaf are easily answered with similar sorts of foliage a little distance away on

Water-lilies bear leaves which, in their quiet, stately way, are as beautiful as any others. The balance between leaf elegance and floral flamboyance is perfect.

drier ground. Many grasses like dry conditions and will continue the theme set in the water, and water irises have their dry-land counterparts as well. *Iris laevigata* forms can bestride the transition from water to wet soil, while *I. chrysographes* and *I. forrestii* and their hybrids take similar leaves and a range of colours from deep purple to straw-yellow right up the bank.

The arrow-head leaves of *Sagittaria* can be linked back, in shape if not in size, to *Arum italicum* var. *pictum*. This smaller plant has spear-shaped leaves heavily marbled in cream and light grey-green. The leaves are formed in autumn and are present throughout the winter, meeting those of the arrow-head for a time in spring and early summer before they die off, leaving behind bright red berries on rather surprised-looking stalks.

Distinct from *Arum italicum* var. *pictum* but the plant that most people think of as an 'arum lily' is *Zantedeschia aethiopica*. With a name like this, no wonder it continues to be called 'arum lily'! This will grow either with its collar in water or as a plant of less wet slopes, whereas the little marbled arum will not tolerate wetness. The spear shape is present very strongly in the leaves and will carry on right through the summer. Indeed, in mild places it is evergreen and its noble, upright clumps of light green are a brave sight on a misty winter's day. It is astonishingly salt-tolerant and could be seen growing in the harbour wall of the little village of Mousehole, in Cornwall, where Atlantic gales thrash the sea just outside its shelter. Where winters are colder, it is as well to grow it with its collar below ice-level if possible, although really cold places will be too much for it. They may even be too harsh for the form *Z.a.* 'Crowborough', but they would have to be severe indeed to be so. This plant will grow right away from any water in a sunny border provided that it is well protected for its first few winters, and can provide a thread linking the water to the drier, more upland parts of the garden.

Rock gardens

In Nature a rock garden will consist of an outcrop of rock – it may be only a metre or so across or it may be a substantial part of a mountain – that abuts grassy or more sheltered areas or richer

LEFT A water feature in a small garden, in which the maximum use of available space has been made. The essential restfulness of water gardens has been preserved, even though there are many plants to be seen. There is no air of busy-ness, but the opportunity has been taken to establish a marginal population that contrasts with the water-lilies and hints at the drier conditions beyond.

RIGHT The marbled, arrow-head leaves of Arum italicum *var.* pictum.

FAR RIGHT A plant like this makes it hard to understand those who would do away with flowers in their gardens and grow nothing but 'foliage plants'. Zantedeschia aethiopica *has no rival for sheer stateliness – a quality derived from its foliage as well as its flowers. It is also quite hardy if its collar is below ice-level, and the variety 'Crowborough' is hardier still.*

places where plants can grow to be much larger than their saxatile neighbours.

Almost by definition the foliage of a rock garden is part of the lower layer. A good, well-made, mature rock garden will display a great deal of foliage, since most alpine plants are evergreen (deciduousness being an unnecessary attribute in a small plant that is covered snugly by dry snow during the very long Cold). The overall effect of a well-planted rock garden will be one of cushions and pads of greys, greens and golds, all happily jostling one another as they nestle down below the harshest winds.

So often, however, the rock garden is a 'rockery', obtrusive as a sore thumb and made the more so because of the neat, plantless area that surrounds it. Integrating it into the garden scene does not mean making it part of the general flowering melee but of the lower layer of foliage. Very simply, for example, this may be achieved by allowing the heathers that cling to the hem of a eucryphia to peter out among the coarser alpines, as the incoming tide, its watery fingers probing, laps up to a rock pool and, merging with it, establishes it as part of the sea.

Peat gardens

The peat bed, or peat garden, that playground of the specialist and of those who have found the esoteric delights that it affords endlessly fascinating, is even easier to present as just one organ of the body horticultural. The dwarf rhododendrons, the cassiopes, andromedas and gaultherias that love it so much are naturally and properly made for associating with their larger counterparts and cousins in the great family of the Ericaceae. Indeed, looking at it the other way round, what better way is there of bordering a plantation of larger rhododendrons, pieris and azaleas than with peat beds in which the ultra-fine root systems of the dwarf plants can settle happily?

Rhododendrons, whose foliage is an eleven-month presence, have indeed a succession of flowering, but each one is barren for all but that one month and, if it is large, presents a profile like that of a parachute – all canopy above and rather stringy beneath. To fill the gap with smaller species, graduating to the dwarfs, accompanied at the lowest level by other denizens of cool, leafy dampness, is to create a scene of great beauty for the simple ingredients of green leaves.

Leaf Shapes and Margins

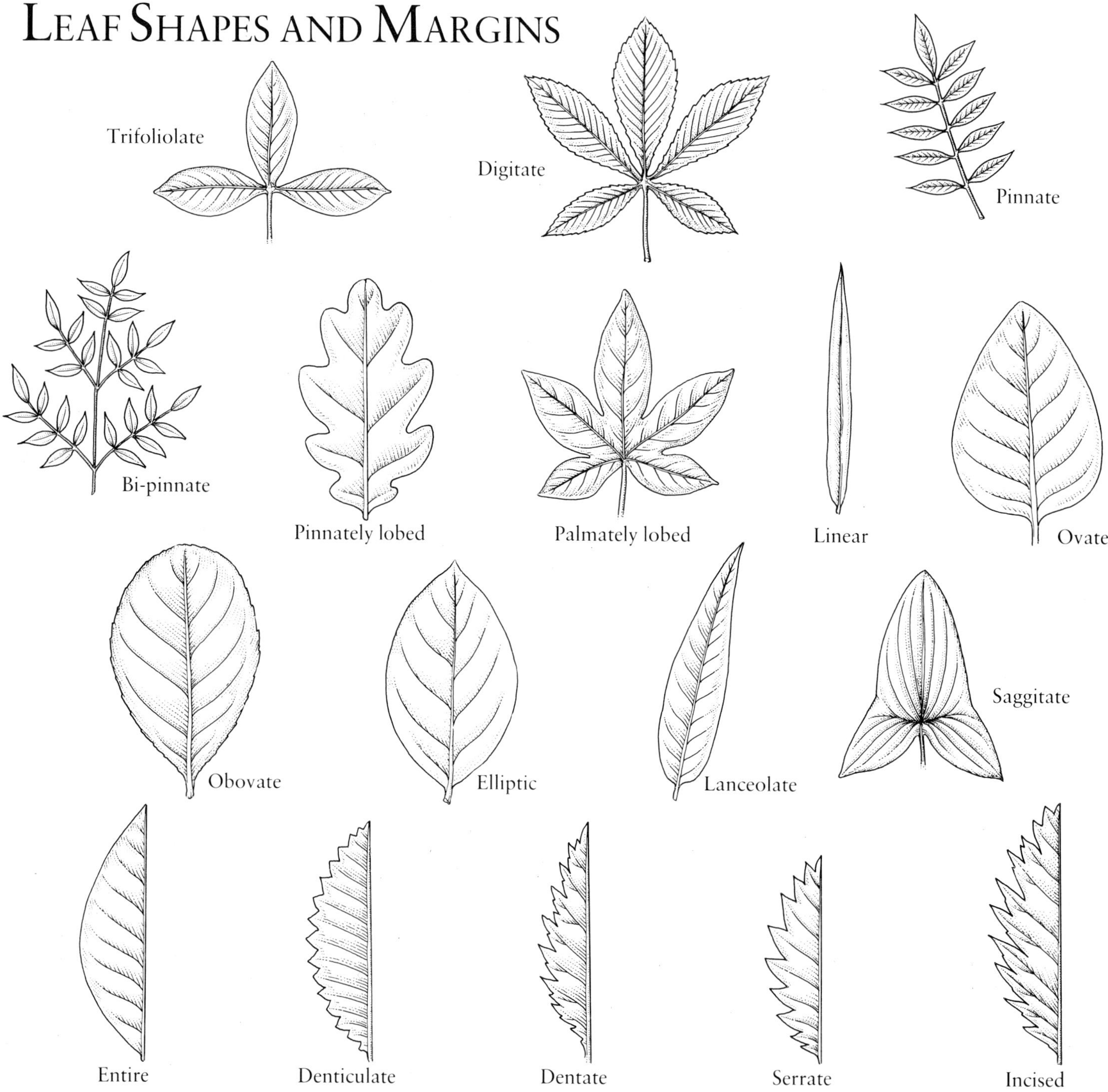

Recommended Plants

E = Evergreen B = Bamboo F = Fern

Large or Bold Foliage

Trees and Shrubs

Aesculus indica
A. parviflora
A. splendens
Aralia elata
A.e. 'Aureovariegata'
A.e. 'Variegata'
Catalpa bignonioides
C.b. 'Aurea'
Eriobotrya japonica E
Fatsia japonica E
F.j. 'Variegata' E
Gymnocladus dioica
Hedera colchica 'Dentata Variegata' E
Idesia polycarpa
Kalopanax pictus
Koelreuteria paniculata
Liriodendron tulipifera
Magnolia grandiflora E
M. macrophylla
M. × soulangiana
M. tripetala
Mahonia japonica E
M. lomariifolia E
M. × media 'Charity' E
M. × m. 'Winter Sun' E
Paeonia lutea var. *ludlowii*
Parrotia persica
Parthenocissus quinquefolia
Paulownia tomentosa
Photinia 'Red Robin' E
Picea brewerana E
Populus lasiocarpa
P. wilsonii
Quercus aliena
Q. castaneifolia
Q. frainetto
Q. palustris
Rhododendron arboreum E
R. calophytum E
R. macabeanum E
R. sinogrande E
Rhus typhina
R.t. 'Dissecta'
Sorbus aria 'Lutescens'
Wisteria floribunda
W. sinensis
Yucca filamentosa E
Y. gloriosa E
Y. recurvifolia E

Perennials

Cyclamen hederifolium
Dryopteris berreri EF
Gunnera manicata
Hosta albomarginata
H. crispula
H. decorata
H. fortunei
H. sieboldiana
H.s. var. *elegans*
H. 'Thomas Hogg'
Kirengeshoma palmata
Matteuccia struthiopteris F
Miscanthus sacchariflorus
Osmunda regalis F
Peltiphyllum peltatum
Phormium tenax E
P.t. 'Variegatum' E
Phyllitis scolopendrium EF
Polygonatum giganteum
P. × hybridum
Rodgersia tabularis
Sagittaria sagittifolia
Veratrum nigrum

Dense Foliage

Trees and Shrubs

Abies pinsapo E
A.p. 'Glauca' E
A. procera 'Glauca Prostrata' E
Arbutus unedo E
Arundinaria nitida E B
Berberis darwinii E
Camellia japonica cultivars E
Carpinus betulus 'Columnaris'
C.b. 'Fastigiata'
Cedrus libani E
Chamaecyparis lawsoniana E
C.l. 'Intertexta' E
C.l. 'Lane' E
C.l. 'Lutea' E
C.l 'Pembury Blue' E
C.l 'Triomf van Boskoop' E
Choisya ternata E
Colletia armata E
Cryptomeria japonica E
× *Cupressocyparis leylandii* E
Cupressus macrocarpa 'Donard Gold' E
C.m. 'Lutea' E
Erica arborea E
Fagus sylvatica 'Dawyck'
Fraxinus excelsior 'Pendula'
Lonicera nitida 'Baggesen's Gold' E
Mahonia japonica E
M. lomariifolia E
M. × media 'Charity' E
M. × m. 'Winter Sun' E
Phyllostachys viridi-glaucescens E B
Picea pungens var. *glauca* E
P.p. 'Koster' E
Pittosporum tenuifolium 'Abbotsbury Gold' E
Prunus cerasifera 'Pissardii'
Quercus ilex E

Gold Foliage

Trees and Shrubs

Catalpa bignonioides 'Aurea'
Chamaecyparis lawsoniana 'Lane' E
C.l. 'Lutea' E
Cupressus macrocarpa 'Donard Gold' E
C.m. 'Lutea' E
Fagus sylvatica 'Aurea Pendula'
F.s. 'Zlatia'
Gleditsia triacanthos 'Sunburst'
Hedera helix 'Buttercup' E
Ilex aquifolium 'Ferox Aurea' E
Lonicera nitida 'Baggesen's Gold' E
Philadelphus coronarius 'Aureus'
Pittosporum tenuifolium 'Abbotsbury Gold' E
Populus × canadensis 'Serotina Aurea'
Quercus robur 'Concordia'
Robinia pseudoacacia 'Frisia'

Grey, Silver or Blue Foliage

Trees and Shrubs

Abies pinsapo 'Glauca' E
A. procera 'Glauca Prostrata' E
Cedrus atlantica var. *glauca* E
Chamaecyparis lawsoniana 'Pembury Blue' E
C.l. 'Triomf van Boskoop' E
Convolvulus cneorum E

Cytisus battandieri
Eucalyptus coccifera E
E. gunnii E
Hebe pinguifolia 'Pagei' E
H. rakaiensis E
Lavandula stoechas
Picea pungens var. *glauca* E
P.p. 'Koster' E
Romneya coulteri
Rosa rubrifolia
Sorbus aria 'Lutescens'

Perennials
Anaphalis triplinervis
A. yedoensis
Artemisia ludoviciana var. *latiloba*
Festuca amethystina E
F. glauca E
Helictotrichon sempervirens E
Hosta sieboldiana
H.s. var. *elegans*
Olearia macrodonta E
Salvia argentea

Red or Copper Foliage

Trees and Shrubs
Acer platanoides 'Crimson King'
A. pseudoplatanus 'Atropurpureum' (syn. 'Spaethii')
Cotinus coggygria
C. 'Grace'
C. 'Notcutt's Purple'
C. 'Velvet Cloak'
Erica carnea 'Vivellii' E
Fagus sylvatica 'Rohanii'
Fuchsia magellanica 'Versicolor'
Photinia 'Red Robin' E
Pieris 'Forest Flame' E
Populus × canadensis 'Serotina'
Prunus cerasifera 'Pissardii'

Perennial
Ligularia 'Desdemona'

Variegated Foliage

Trees and Shrubs
Acer platanoides 'Drummondii'
Aralia elata 'Aureovariegata'
A.e. 'Variegata'
Cornus alba 'Elegantissima'
C.a. 'Spaethii'
C. controversa 'Variegata'
Elaeagnus pungens 'Dicksonii' E
E.p. 'Maculata' E
Euonymus fortunei 'Variegatus' E
Fatsia japonica 'Variegata' E
Fuchsia magellanica 'Variegata'
F.m. 'Versicolor'
Hedera colchica 'Dentata Variegata' E
H. helix 'Buttercup' E
H.h. 'Gold Heart' E
Hydrangea 'Quadricolor'
Ilex × altaclarensis 'Golden King' E
I. aquifolium 'Ferox Argentea' E
I.a. 'Golden Milkboy' E
I.a. 'Golden Queen' E
I.a. 'Handsworth New Silver' E
I.a. 'Silver Queen' E
Osmanthus heterophyllus 'Variegatus' E
Pieris japonica 'Variegata' E

Perennials
Acorus calamus 'Variegatus'
Brunnera macrophylla 'Hadspen Cream'
B.m. 'Langtrees'
B.m. 'Variegata'
Convallaria majalis 'Variegata'
Cyclamen hederifolium
Hosta albomarginata
H. crispula
H. 'Thomas Hogg'
Iris pallida 'Variegata'
I. pseudacorus 'Variegata'
Phlox paniculata 'Norah Leigh'
Phormium tenax 'Variegatum' E
P. 'Yellow Wave' E
Polygonatum japonicum 'Variegatum'
Pulmonaria saccharata E
Symphytum × uplandicum 'Variegatum'

Autumn Colour

Trees and Shrubs
Acer capillipes
A. circinatum
A. palmatum 'Dissectum'
A.p. 'Senkaki'
A. pensylvanicum
A. platanoides 'Crimson King'
A. rubrum 'October Glory'
Aesculus indica
A. parviflora
A. splendens
Betula ermanii
B. jacquemontii
B. luminifera
B. papyrifera
B. utilis
Fothergilla monticola
Ginkgo biloba
Gymnocladus dioica
Liquidambar styraciflua
Liriodendron tulipifera
Parrotia persica
Parthenocissus quinquefolia
Quercus aliena
Rhododendron luteum
Rhus typhina
R.t. 'Dissecta'

Leaves of Unusual Shape

Trees and Shrubs
Acer palmatum 'Dissectum'
Colletia armata E
Decaisnea fargesii
Fagus sylvatica 'Asplenifolia'
F.s. 'Zlatia'
Ficus carica
Ginkgo biloba
Idesia polycarpa
Ilex aquifolium 'Ferox' E
I.a. 'Ferox Argentea' E
I.a. 'Ferox Aurea' E
I. pernyi E
Kalopanax pictus
Koelreuteria paniculata
Liriodendron tulipifera
Magnolia tripetala
Mahonia lomariifolia E
M. × media 'Charity' E
M. × m. 'Winter Sun' E
Quercus castaneifolia
Q. frainetto
Q. hispanica 'Lucombeana' E
Rhus typhina 'Dissecta'

Perennials
Alchemilla mollis
Phormium 'Yellow Wave' E
Veratrum nigrum

Plant Index

Page numbers in **bold** refer to illustrations

R

S

T

V

W

Y

Z

Useful Addresses

The Aberconwy Nurseries
Graig, Glan Conwy, Clwyd LL28 7TL
(Perennials, conifers, trees and shrubs)

* **David Austin Roses**
Bowling Green Lane, Albrighton, Wolverhampton WV7 3HB
(Old-fashioned rose specialists)

Bressingham Nurseries Ltd.
Bressingham, Diss, Norfolk IP22 2AB
(Wide range of herbaceous plants and conifers, ferns, grasses and bamboos)

Peter Chappell
Spinners, Boldre, Lymington, Hants SO41 5QE
(Wide range of unusual plants)

* **Beth Chatto**
Elmstead Market, Colchester, Essex CO7 7DB
(Unusual plant specialist, mainly herbaceous)

* **Chiltern Seeds**
Bartree Stile, Ulverton, Cumbria LA12 7PB
(Huge range of unusual plants from seed of all kinds)

* **Jack Drake**
Inshriach, Aviemore, Inverness PH22 1QS
(Alpine specialist with good range of heathers)

* MAIL-ORDER SERVICE AVAILABLE

* **Glendoick Gardens Ltd.**
Glencarse, Perth PH2 7NS
(Rhododendron specialist; azaleas and other *Ericaceae)*

Hayes Garden World
Lake Road, Ambleside, Cumbria, OA22 ODW
(First-class, comprehensive garden centre)

* **Hillier Nurseries (Winchester) Ltd.**
Ampfield House, Ampfield, Nr Romsey, Hants SO51 9PA
(The most comprehensive list of trees and shrubs of all kinds)

* **Kelways Nurseries**
Langport, Somerset TA10 9SL
(A wide range of herbaceous plants)

Mallett Court Nursery
Curry Mallet, Taunton, Somerset TA3 6SY
(Unusual trees, including many *Quercus* and *Acer*)

The National Trust
Bodnant, Tal-y-Cafn, Clwyd LL28 5RE
(Trees, shrubs, rhododendrons, azaleas)

* **Ramparts Nurseries**
Bakers Lane, Colchester, Essex CO4 5BB
(Silver and grey foliage plants)

* **G Reuthe Ltd.**
Sevenoaks Road, Ightham, Kent TN15 0BH
(Unusual shrubs, trees, conifers, rhododendrons, heathers)

Royal Horticultural Society
Wisley, Ripley, Woking, Surrey GU23 6QB
(All kinds of unusual plants)

* **St Bridget Nurseries**
Old Rydon Lane, Exeter, Devon EX2 7JY
(Shrubs, trees, climbers, some shrub roses, herbaceous plants, rhododendrons)

* **Sherrards**
The Garden Centre, Wantage Road, Donnington, Newbury, Berks RG18 9BE
(Unusual trees, shrubs and climbers, herbaceous plants, old-fashioned roses)

* **Southcombe Gardens Plant Nursery**
Widecombe-in-the-Moor, Newton Abbot, Devon TQ13 7TU
(Unusual plants including shrubs, trees, border plants, grasses, heathers)

* **Starborough Nursery**
Starborough Road, Marsh Green, Edenbridge, Kent TN8 5RB
(High-quality trees and shrubs, including many excellent ones for foliage)

Acknowledgments

Publishers' Acknowledgments
The publishers would like to thank the following individuals for their help in producing this book: Yvonne Cummerson and Louise Tucker for their help with design work and Susanne Haines for initial editorial work. Thanks also to Paul Meyer and Joanna Chisholm for their help with the American edition, to Tony Lord for the index, Katy Foskew for clerical help and to Chris Myers at Bookworm for burning the midnight oil.

Special thanks to Mr and Mrs Chappel and to John Hilton for permission to photograph their gardens.

Editors Jo Christian, Barbara Vesey
Art Editor Bob Gordon
Picture Researcher Anne Fraser

Typesetting
Set in Linotron Sabon by Bookworm Typesetting, Manchester, England

Origination
Evergreen Colour Separation Co. Ltd, Hong Kong

Illustrators
Cover border by Michael Craig
Leaf shapes and margins on page 136 by Sandra Pond

Photographers
L=left R=right B=bottom T=top

Tony Bates 14, 37, 46, 72, 98, 123B
Geoff Dann 2, 19 ©FLL, 20 ©FLL, 23, 24 ©FLL, 26, 31©FLL, 36 © FLL, 43 © FLL, 49, 58 © FLL, 64 © FLL, 76B © FLL, 81T © FLL, 97T © FLL, 104 © FLL, 108 © FLL, 112, 115T © FLL, 117B © FLL, 118B © FLL, 119 © FLL, 120T, 127 © FLL
Arnaud Descat 11, 101
Inge Espen-Hansen 40, 71
Derek Fell 8, 81B, 88B, 89
John Glover 18L, 18R, 39, 51, 60, 63L, 63R, 67, 68, 76T, 79T, 82, 86R, 87, 100T, 100B, 132, 134
Jerry Harpur 30
Marijke Heuff 1, 21, 22, 35, 41, 44, 47, 85, 96T, 110, 113, 114
Jacqui Hurst 7, 12 © FLL, 27 © FLL, 105 © FLL, 126 © FLL
John Kelly 118T
Andrew Lawson 52, 61, 78, 79B, 90, 103, 106, 107, 121B, 123T, 124, 125, 130, 131, 133, 135L, 135R
Georges Lévêque 34 © FLL
Natural Image/Robin Fletcher 66, 75, 84, 94, 96B, 97B, 120B, 122
Natural Image/Bob Gibbons 50, 53, 62, 74, 88T, 121T
Natural Image/Liz Gibbons 57, 128
Natural Image/Peter Wilson 117T
Photos Horticultural/Michael Warren 16R, 59, 80, 86L, 91, 93, 95, 99, 102, 109, 115B, 116, 129
Gary Rogers 25
Ianthe Ruthven 17 (Designer: Arabella Lennox-Boyd)
Harry Smith/Horticultural Photographic Collection 48, 54, 55, 69T, 69B
Ron Sutherland 15 ©FLL
Steve Wooster 16L, 28, 29, 32, 33, 77